April 16,

Ken & Helen

love + best wishes

Jack

# CATHOLIC CHURCH?
# WHY NOT?
## Diaries of a Modern Priest

## Jack Scissons

### Volume II

**author**HOUSE

*AuthorHouse™*
*1663 Liberty Drive*
*Bloomington, IN 47403*
*www.authorhouse.com*
*Phone: 833-262-8899*

*© 2023 Jack Scissons. All rights reserved.*

*No part of this book may be reproduced, stored in a retrieval system, or transmitted by any means without the written permission of the author.*

*Published by AuthorHouse  03/30/2023*

*ISBN: 979-8-8230-0387-2 (sc)*
*ISBN: 979-8-8230-0386-5 (hc)*
*ISBN: 979-8-8230-0388-9 (e)*

*Library of Congress Control Number: 2023904997*

*Print information available on the last page.*

*Any people depicted in stock imagery provided by Getty Images are models, and such images are being used for illustrative purposes only.*
*Certain stock imagery © Getty Images.*

*This book is printed on acid-free paper.*

*Because of the dynamic nature of the Internet, any web addresses or links contained in this book may have changed since publication and may no longer be valid. The views expressed in this work are solely those of the author and do not necessarily reflect the views of the publisher, and the publisher hereby disclaims any responsibility for them.*

"Never doubt that a small group of thoughtful committed citizens can change the world; indeed, it is the only thing that ever has."
Margaret Mead (1901-1978)

"The Church must be a place of mercy freely given, where everyone can feel welcomed, loved, forgiven and encouraged to live the good life of the Gospel."
Pope Francis (2013 -)

**IN APPRECIATION**

The author would like to thank the staff at Author House for their assistance, patience and advice on guiding him through the process of writing and publishing this book, especially Eve Ardell, Jamaica Delfin, Cleo Carrigan, Blake Preston, Charmaine Bolton, Jorie Reff, Josh Laluna, Nolan Estes, but especially Mae Genson, Senior Publishing Consultant-Supervisor.

    A special thank you to Kathleen my wife for her patience with my endless need to edit.

## CONTENTS

Introduction ................................................................... ix

Chapter 1   Journal Entries for November ........................... 1
Chapter 2   Journal Entries for December ......................... 73
Chapter 3   Journal Entries for January ........................... 118
Chapter 4   Journal Entries for February ......................... 174
Monthly Reports to the Vatican ....................................... 237

Acknowledgements ........................................................ 251
Recommended Readings ............................................... 253

## INTRODUCTION

This volume continues with the daily journals of Father Cam Walker begun in Volume I. It records his daily routine, the issues and the challenges of a newly-ordained formerly-married Catholic priest. In his first parish assignment, he struggles with reconciling Christ's teachings to love, to forgive and not to judge with the discriminatory teachings of the Catholic Church regarding women, women priests, married priests, divorce, birth control, abortion, doctor assisted dying and LGBTQS+ men and women. His protestant colleagues challenge him too.

He still thinks with sadness of his wife Wendy who died of ALS. Why did God take her when she was such a kind and caring professional marriage counselor? What was he supposed to learn from the loss of her? He still remembers with grave regret his alcoholic period after she died and grateful to the Benedictine treatment center that saved his life. He worries that he has not heard any reaction to the article that Ed Malone wrote about Bishop Ben and him for the Toronto Tribune. Is no news in this situation good news?

Note:

The language of the Bible refers to God as masculine or as a he. God is neither male nor female. God is non-binary. The Bible was written when patriarchy was prevalent and men exclusively were the leaders in society. Women played only a secondary role at that time. Unfortunately, we do not yet have the English vocabulary that properly describes who God is.

## LIST OF CHARACTERS

Cardinal George, the Archbishop of Toronto;

Bishop Ben (and his rescue dog Max) the leader of a Catholic Diocese in Western Canada;

Father Cam Walker, newly ordained Parish Priest of St Francis and St. Joseph Parishes in Bishop Ben's Diocese;

Father Mike Thomas, St. Patrick's Parish, (Father Cam's first parish assignment);

Father Joe, a Benedictine monk (advisor and friend);

Father Tim Ryan, (pedophile) St George's Parish (in Bishop Ben's diocese);

Royal Canadian Mounted Police: Sergeant Ron Walker and Constable Melanie Campbell;

Town Hospital: Dr. Tom Hazelton and Nurse Rita White;

Samaritan Club: Jerome Nesbit and Raymond LeBois (two gay men in a long-term relationship);

Parish Council: Fred and Thelma Bartlett, Ned and Mabel Armstrong, Bill and Liz McMillan, Jim and Trudy Truman, Mario and Isabella DeMarco, Tom and Ann McCaffrey, Colin and Marion McNeil;

Catholic Women's Association (CWA) a parish women's organization that is part of a national Catholic women's organization: Mabel Armstrong, Thelma Bartlett, Liz McMillan, Trudy Truman, Isabella DeMarco, Ann McCaffrey and Marion McNeil;

Men's Club is a parish men's club that supports the men of the parish and contributes to the community: Fred Bartlett, Ned Armstrong, Bill McMillan, Jim Truman, Mario DeMarco, Tom McCaffrey and Colin McNeil;

Interdenominational Group: Rev. Claire Meadows (Anglican), Don Keating (Buddhist), Rev. Joan White (United Church), Peter Smith (Just curious) and Ed Malone (Editor, Prairie News) (a local weekly newspaper));

A Priest support group called a Deanery: It includes Fathers George West from St. Mary's Parish; Mark de Santos from Holy Family Parish; Raj Patel from St. Thomas Parish and Ted Hazelton from Holy Angels Parish;

Lawyer: Paul Taylor and his wife Simone;

Unwanted pregnancies: Susan (from Australia) and Maggie Taylor (Paul's daughter);

Todd Joseph (Town Manager), Stanley Robinson (retired City Planner), William Blake, (Town Engineer), Mary Jones, (Town Secretary);

Ed Malone, editor of the local newspaper, "Prairie News" and wife Elaine (Nurse)

# CHAPTER 1

# *Journal Entries for November*

---

### Monday, November 1—Day off

Mantra for the day:

God told Abram: "Leave your country, your family and your father's home for a land that I will show you. I'll make you a great nation and bless you. I will make you famous; you'll be a blessing to others. I will bless those who bless you; those who curse you, I'll curse. All the families of the earth will be blessed through you."
(Book of Genesis, ch. 12, v. 1–3)

I was having a leisurely breakfast with Mother at 9:00 a.m. when Bishop Ben called. After the usual pleasantries, he requested a meeting with Father Mike and me. When could I arrive in his office? I responded in thirty minutes. He agreed and hung up. Mother quietly inquired if I there was a problem but I assured her that everything was fine. Then Ed Malone called to request a meeting. He agreed to meet me at the rectory with pizza at 6:00 p.m.; Elaine was on night shift at the hospital.

    Margaret ushered me into the Bishop's office to an exuberant tail-wagging welcome from Max, the Bishop's dog. Father Mike was already there. The welcome from both the Bishop and Father Mike were tame by comparison. I immediately became concerned; was I being ambushed here? Margaret arrived with a cup of coffee to my usual specifics after the greetings subsided. She is a mind reader. Women that are mind readers are dangerous. Max got my attention with his demands for a hug and a back rub. The Bishop began by thanking us for making ourselves available on such short notice and on your day off, Father Cam. The Bishop continued by saying that Ed Malone's article in the *Toronto Tribune* about us—Father Cam and I had gained a lot of traction over the last few days. Cardinal George had phoned him to say that he did not want to be blindsided by news. The Cardinal wanted me to keep him well informed in advance of newsworthy church items. The Cardinal said that he would be forwarding the article to the Vatican's representative in Canada, Archbishop Benevento. By the way, Archbishop Benevento requested the names of three priests who have future bishop potential. The Bishop assured us that this was normal practice. The Church is always looking for candidates for leadership positions both in Canada and in Rome. "I am considering putting forward the names of Father Derek Hildebrand and the two of you, Father Mike, and you too, Father Cam." He then asked us for our reaction. Father Mike thanked the Bishop for the vote of confidence but felt his weak heart and diabetes precluded him from accepting this responsibility. He went on at some length, elaborating on how the stress of his age at sixty-nine and health problems would probably kill him. Bishop Ben assured Father Mike that he would not recommend him for those reasons. "Father Mike, you are known as very kind and considerate, and your parishioners love your calm manner. Remember Pope John

XXIII was also an older man when he became Pope, and look what he accomplished. You are my first choice, but I will include in your profile all your personal health concerns."

He then looked at me. Like Father Mike, I thanked him for considering me but told him that I am not ready for such responsibilities. I did not want to be disobedient or unappreciative, but I am still very inexperienced and still very busy with the work program that we devised for the parish last July. I am still establishing relationships in the parishes. The Bishop then said that Hildebrand was unable to be present today, but he will be meeting him tomorrow. He continued that he was required to create a "watch list" for the Vatican, and he would include Father Mike's reservations and my lack of readiness given my recent ordination to the priesthood. He reminded me that my age, my former marriage, and my previous employment experience were great assets.

As I left his office, Bishop Ben inquired if I was still going to spend Wednesday to Friday with the Benedictines. I replied that as soon as I completed my scripture course tomorrow I would drive up. Father Joe would wait up for me. He ended our conversation by saying that next time he would like to come along. I invited him to join me and to just come for a day to try out their hospitality.

Ed arrived at 6:00 p.m. with two bottles of Sangiovese and a couple of Mario's pizzas with pepperoni, basil, extra tomato, hot peppers, and extra cheese. He seemed very excited, but I could not tell what excited him more—the food or our visit. He began by saying that he had received a lot of good feedback on the *Toronto Tribune* article. The Cardinal had phoned Ed on Saturday morning as he was reading the column, and the Cardinal sounded impressed—both with Ed's writing ability and his favorable and objective comments on me and the Bishop. He then asked me if I thought that Bishop Ben was promotable, which caught me totally off guard and speechless. He reminded me that the Vatican discovered Bishop Ben as a young priest working in Ecuador and promoted him. Ed liked the fact that Bishop Ben is down to earth, lives a simple lifestyle, and walks everywhere. He hypothesized that he gets a lot of attention because of his dog, Max. I asked Ed if he had met Max.

"Oh, yes, sticky tennis ball and all."

I boldly asked Ed if he was Catholic. After an awkward silence, he admitted that he was not a practicing Catholic. To my obvious follow-up question, he responded by saying that his Catholic practice, or lack thereof, has a long story and he would save the details for another dinner of pizza and wine. He continued that the Cardinal asked about you, Father Cam. Ed elaborated to him what you Father Cam have done in this parish in the last four months especially the Community Volunteer Appreciation Night and the Inter-denominational group.

Ed continued, "What are your plans for the days ahead? Can we open the second bottle of wine and order more pizza while you outline your plans for the months ahead?"

I took a deep breath and outlined the immediate actions that I foresee in the months ahead; we need to flesh out the details for the following: the park's maintenance program for the town and getting our teens involved in it; we need to develop a youth service program that will work to develop clean water, housing and soccer fields in Central America; a marriage renewal weekend for couples in the two parishes where the talks will be given by the married couples themselves; the Good Samaritan Club have agreed to a cooking course for the men of the parish; the local CWA thinks the Town needs a women and girls softball league. Other issues will pop up as we continue to journey as a parish community. Again, I asked him if he had any suggestions on how the parish can serve the community.

He asked me, "Have you heard of Marshall McLuhan?"

"No, I had not".

He continued that in his communications class at Ryerson, they studied him. McLuhan is a well-known Eastern academic. He coined a phrase that characterizes his work "the medium is the message". The medium (how the message is distributed) can be more important than the message. Community service programs for youth would be a good example of Christianity in action. Ed continued that we have moved from information in newspapers to TV to computers and electronic devices of all kinds. He said that he was raising this because he had heard me express on a number of occasions that the young people have abandoned the Church and how concerned I was. Do you think it might be the medium the Church was using?

Ed then asked if I had heard the latest town news?

"No," I replied.

"The Province and the Mayor think our town would be a good location for a chicken processing plant and they are in active negotiations regarding the location and other related services like housing, walkable commercial uses, more doctors and nurses, a hospital addition."

I was blown away.

He continued, with your background in affordable housing and emergency housing for women, would you agree to join an advisory committee of Town Council? I assured him that I would if and when asked. He agreed to pass my work experience along to the Town office. After Ed had consumed most of the second bottle of wine, he began to tell me stories of his work in the Italian community in Toronto. He left at 9:00 pm.

No soon after his departure, I began to worry that my personal conversations with Ed were going straight to his friend the Cardinal in Toronto. I cannot be secretive in this job nevertheless chatting with Ed could be a risk. I then, emailed the Bishop with Ed's town's news and my suspicion that Ed was having regular communications with the Cardinal. My hunch that the subject of such chatter is both of us. Bishop Ben, I sincerely hope that I am not getting you into trouble with your brother bishops. I also invited him again to join me on my Benedictine retreat even for one day, perhaps, Friday. All the gardening work at the Monastery would be finished for the year and the food would be the freshest. A few minutes later, my laptop binged. He replied saying that he will not know for sure until after he meets with Margaret in the morning. He also said that he will be bringing Max. Max is so well behaved that he will be fine in the guest quarters and even in the Monastery. The Benedictine's strong belief in hospitality means that they will never turn anyone away, not even Max.

Father in heaven, save me from a Church promotion. I am neither emotionally ready nor trained for a management role. I am very happy working in St. Francis. My university education and my employment experience are more suited for this parish, at least for the next few years. Today is the feast of All Saints Day, when we recognize all the good people who have lived before us. Thank you, Father, in heaven for Bishop Ben, Father Mike, the priests of the diocese, my family and the parishioners of St. Francis and St. Joseph's. Keep them in your love.

## Tuesday, November 2
## Personal study Benedictine Spirituality

Mantra for the Day:

"Blessed are those that are merciful and care for others, for they shall be shown mercy." (Gospel of Matthew, ch. 5, v. 7)

I skipped out of my scripture course today preferring to making notes on Benedictine spirituality. The course content today was to be the understanding and use of Greek in the Bible. I think studying Benedictine spirituality could be more productive and helpful for future Sunday homilies.

## Summary notes:

1. St Benedict (480 – 547 of the Common Era [C.E.]) is known as the founder of the Benedictines (OSB) and the founder of Western Monasticism, but he was not the first Christian monk. OSB stands for the Order of St. Benedict;
2. When the Romans destroyed Jerusalem and the Temple, the centre of Christianity in 70 CE, the apostles and disciples who comprised the early Christians, were dispersed throughout the Middle East;
3. Christians were also persecuted particularly in Rome because they refused to honor the Roman deities of the time;
4. Men and women, known as the desert fathers and mothers, became the custodians of the early phases of monastic living from 100 to 300 CE. They moved to the desert (Egypt) and Syria to avoid persecution and to discover their spiritual paths. Some lived as hermits in caves while others lived in small groups dedicated to prayer and charitable works. The small groups were the preferred type of St Basil the Great (330- 379 CE) and St John Cassian (360 – 435 CE), two larger than life Church leaders in monastic living at the time;
5. The rise of Monasticism coincided with the fall of Rome in 395 - 476 CE;
6. This period of history was fraught with political, economic and social chaos from Gaul (as France was then known) to Syria. There was little security or certainty. The Christian Church was as troubled as the secular powers. Life was confusing and hard to make sense of.

7. Benedict of Nursia was born into this period of upheaval. His public life began with studies in Rome but he abandoned them before completion. He left Rome and moved to nearby Subiaco where he lived the life of a hermit in a cave for three years. He was probably 20 years of age at the time. Later, he began organizing small groups of monks (approximately 12 in size) to live and work together. This experience was successful and lasted about 25 years. In 525 CE, a dispute led him to leave and move with a group of monks to Monte Cassino (a mountain south of Rome) where they built a new monastery;
8. Benedict's type of monasticism was a community of brothers living and working together who regularly selected their leader, the Abbot, who represented a loving father. Benedict emphasized the horizontal rather than the vertical relationships in the monastery. Successful monasteries needed all the necessities of life such as a water supply, fruit and vegetable gardens and the practice of crafts to survive and to support themselves financially.
9. It was near the end of his life that he wrote his rule, based in part on an existing Rule, called "The Rule of the Master";
10. Benedict's rule was known as being moderate, humane and short. It envisions a community of men and women dedicated to following Christ and sharing all in common as did the first disciples of Christ;
11. Each Benedictine community is self-sufficient and autonomous;
12. Daily prayer (Opus Dei), daily reading and reflection of the Bible (Lectio Divina) and work are at the core of monastic life;

13. From 500 to 1500 CE, the monastic ideals advocated by Benedict have been a foundation of the rebuilding and the stabilization of Europe;
14. Key teachings are stability (comfort in living in a particular place), prayer, work, hospitality and obedience to the rule.

Tuesday night: I arrived at 8:00 pm at the monastery. Father Joe was waiting up for me. He took me to the kitchen for a bowl of curried soup comprised of veggies and lentils along with cheese and Russian bread. Too late to talk. He loaned me a cowl (the Benedictine habit), showed me to my cubicle, had assigned me to kitchen duties for my time at the monastery and advised that I could either sleep in or get up at 5:30 am and join the monks for morning prayer, meditation and mass. The Abbot would like to see you in the morning.

Father in heaven, thank you for another day of living and working with you. It is going to be both fun and exciting to discuss with my friends in the parish how to live out these monastic ideals in their daily lives. Thank you too for the Benedictine hospitality and Father Joe.

## Wednesday -Friday, November 3-5
## My stay with the Benedictines

Mantra for the Day:

"Blessed are you who mourn or when you feel you have lost what is most dear to you, for you will be comforted and will be embraced by the One most dear to you, your heavenly loving Father. (Gospel of Matthew, ch. 5, v. 4)

It feels different back in the monastery, sleeping in the guest quarters. I was going to sleep in but the bell calling everyone to prayer was so loud that I got up too. As a priest, my status has improved over my previous stay when I was a recovering alcoholic. Those persons in treatment live in a bunkhouse, a building separate from the monastery, but take their meals with the monks.

After a breakfast of oatmeal, flax seeds, milk, bread, fruit jam, all produced here at the monastery and of course strong coffee, I found Abbot James and spent a comfortable hour with him. To his question of what the monks could do for me, I replied that I hoped that I could in my brief stay, breathe in their wise spirituality. Parish life can get very busy and often does not allow for structured, regular time for daily prayer and reflection. By the way, I have invited Bishop Ben wants to join us and he may turn up today. He will probably bring his dog, Max, his faithful companion. The Abbot said that he has already phoned to say that he will arrive later today and he has asked Father Joe to be on the lookout for him.

Further to the Abbot's question, I continued, there are probably other priests in my diocese who could benefit from this experience too. The Abbot volunteered that the monks have been wondering of converting the monastery into a retreat house and to offer to preach a retreat for the diocesan priests and the laity of the diocese. He inquired about our parish activities. I briefly outlined my concern that the Church is totally out of touch with Catholics under 40. I furthermore explained that my reading of the Gospel mandate to love, to forgive and to avoid judging one another, seem to be out of synch with the current focus of the Church on divorce, abortion and discriminatory behaviors against women and gays. I described the groups in the parish, the Samaritan Club, working with Susan, Colin and Marion and the challenge that it entails. Some parishioners are very opposed to any type of change in the Church. There are some who still want mass in the Latin language. I personally have not had such a complaint from the parishioners in my parishes, at least not that I know of. He seemed very concerned and understanding.

He again asked what specifically did I think the monks could do for us? I am not sure exactly but as a starting point, you could help us to understand the basics of Benedictine spirituality. Is it not the oldest monastic spirituality? We need to be reminded of the basic Gospel message as it applies to us and our parishioners and secondly, you could become a support group or meditation coaches for parish priests who frequently live and work alone. You might consider attending some of our Deanery meetings to get a better sense of our challenges. We do not need a monastic practice but a spiritual practice geared to a busy lay person. He looked at his watch and noted it was 10:30 am and reminded me that I was needed in the kitchen to help prepare lunch. We agreed to continue our discussion at a later date.

After lunch, the Abbot gave us a short lecture on the benefits of silent meditation where we invite our loving God into our daily routine. A 30-minute quiet meditation would help us see those aspects of ourselves that we avoid and tend to put out of our minds. Carl Jung and Jungian psychologists brilliantly call this behavior of ourselves that we ignore or avoid, our shadow. We do not see our shadow but everyone else does. We think if it is out of mind, we do not have to worry about it. We deceive ourselves. One way of getting to know our shadow is to sit in daily silence where we can observe our minds and emotions.

Wednesday flew by as I blended into the Benedictine daily schedule. Bishop Ben and Max (looking surprisingly comfortable on a leash) arrived in time for dinner and Vespers (evening prayer). His room was next to mine. Max was delighted to see me as usual. He warms my heart.

On Thursday, after morning prayer, meditation, mass and breakfast, I was assigned both to kitchen duties and to table service duties for breakfast, lunch and dinner. As I served the

Abbot his breakfast, he leaned over to Bishop Ben and said in a voice just loud enough for me to hear, that Father Cam was doing the work of three guests, Bishop Ben, Max and Father Cam, as we cannot expect you to do kitchen work and clean toilets on your first visit. They both had a good laugh at my expense. I was glad to see that they were hitting it off. I cannot imagine Bishop Ben cleaning toilets. The Bishop soon caught my eye and said we need to talk alone after breakfast. Where can I find you? I pointed to the Abbot and said ask him. He arrived in the kitchen as I was putting breakfast dishes and cooking utensils into the large commercial dishwasher. I have bad news, Father Patel's Church and rectory burned down late Monday night. It was old, poorly maintained and went down quickly. The half-hour that a nearby volunteer fire department took to arrive on the scene, did not help. While we sort all this out, I have assigned him to live with you. I hope that is OK with you. Bill McMillan has had keys made for him.

Father in heaven, thank you for this wonderful stay. But their beds are way too hard.

Friday: Bishop Ben, Max and I again joined the monks in morning prayer, meditation, mass and breakfast. I then packed my bags and returned to the kitchen for bread making duties and lunch preparation. Lunch was a potato-vegetable soup with monastery made cheese and bread. I thanked the Abbot, Father Joe and Brother John who is in charge of the kitchen, for their hospitality. Father Joe's parting words were that the Abbot had a good visit with me. Bishop Ben, winking at the Abbot, thanked him and me for your hospitality. I later had dinner with my parents and returned home to a TV summary of sports news and my new house guest, Father Raj. He was cleaning up his dinner dishes. The rectory smelled of curry. I showed him around to make him feel welcome. After a short visit, I returned to my office to check on emails and telephone voicemails.

I received a late email from Bishop Ben requesting me to drop everything and come to his office on Saturday morning at

10:00 am. Father Mike will attend too. What kind of trouble am I in now? I wished the Bishop would explain in more detail the nature of these meetings so that I can worry less and properly prepare myself.

Thank you, Father, in heaven for a spiritually energizing week. Keep the Benedictines safe and close to your heart, especially the Abbot, Father Joe, Brother John, the head chef, Father Raj. and his churchless parishioners. Please help me to keep my resolutions to pray and meditate more. As always, thank you for the love and kindness of my parents. Please give me a good night's sleep and not to worry about what the Bishop wants.

## Saturday, November 06
## Meeting with the Bishop

> Mantra for the Day:
>
> "Blessed are the peacemakers that show people how to cooperate instead of competing or fighting, for they will be called children of God and realize their place in God's family." (Gospel of Matthew, ch. 5, v. 9)

I arrived at 9:45 am with my own Starbuck's large coffee. Father Mike had not yet arrived. The Bishop and Max as usual, warmly welcomed me into the office. The Bishop said that Fathers Mike and Hildebrand had phoned and were on route. Max and I got re-acquainted with deep eye-contact, warm kisses, friendly bites and playful tummy rubs. Upon their arrival ten minutes later, the Bishop started by thanking us for attending under short notice. Father Tim Ryan, the parish priest working two rural parishes has been accused by the RCMP of sexually molesting two boys, ages 15 and 13. One incident occurred in his previous parish and the second in his current parish. When the RCMP contacted the Bishop, they thought that the evidence was clear and reliable. They also wanted to know what they should do with this priest. They felt that for his safety, he should not be left in his current parish or in a jail with other inmates. They said that he is scheduled to have a bail hearing next Tuesday and the Crown Prosecutor will be seeking some direction from the Bishop. Regardless of the evidence, for the time being, the Bishop emphasized that he is considered innocent until a Court of Law determines his guilt or innocence. He asked the three of us of our thoughts.

Father Mike began by saying that he has known Father Tim for ten years or more. He is in his mid-sixties, a very kind person but has suffered two previous bouts of alcoholism and spent a month in a Jesuit-run mental hospital allegedly dealing with stress-related issues. He continued that he suspects that Father Tim does not function well living alone in a rural parish. Father Hildebrand expressed his horror with this problem. He has read that there is very little success in the psychological rehabilitation of sex offenders. I suggested that Father Tim should remain in jail until the bail hearing. But after that we need to find him a safe home in the short term while the court determines his guilt or innocence and then in the long term regardless of what the Court determines, he will need a safe place.

I offered a secure room in our local hospital used for violent mental patients where our parishioners could offer solace and assistance. But it is only temporary. I raised my hand with another idea. Bishop, I said, thinking outside the box; the Benedictine's work with alcoholics is slowing down according to Father Joe. Would you consider phoning the Abbot and inquiring if the Monastery would take on sex offenders as a special work program funded by both Federal and Provincial governments? I am one of their success stories, remember? I had a drinking problem. I credit them for turning my life around. The Province or the Federal Government would need to finance the construction of a secure enclosure on the Monastery grounds. This monastery could become a humane secure prison, where these inmates learn to work, to pray and live out their lives with safety and dignity. It could become a model prison. Would you consider consulting your friend, the Cardinal, about this? He just stared at me with that "deer in the headlights" look wondering where you get all these ideas from.

After what seemed like a long silence, the Bishop began saying that while he worries about everyone involved; the boys, the parents, the parishes and the other priests, he is also concerned about the Diocesan finances. We cannot afford an expensive counselling and rehabilitation bill that the Court could level at us.

I said, again thinking outside the box and as a former social worker, that we need to pay whatever it costs to help these boys and their families recover from the damage of this experience. Anything less, would be to re-victimize them. Perhaps we need to consider organizing a Diocesan lottery to pay these difficult expenses. Fathers Mike and Hildebrand looked at me incredulously as if I was the devil incarnate. The Bishop gently replied that the Church historically has not looked favorably on gambling as a way to raise money regardless of the cause. There is a long-standing Catholic moral principle, "the end does not justify the means." At that point, the Bishop got up, indicating the meeting was over. He thanked each of us again for making ourselves available on such short notice. He looked at me and pointed to a chair while he ushered the other two priests from his office.

Sitting across from me, he said that the Anglicans want to take us up on our offer to share our parish Church with them. They would like to use the rectory boardroom for a potluck dinner and then the Church for a liturgy on Sunday evenings. They would begin at 5:00 pm and conclude at 7:30 pm. I offered them the use of our vestments, chalices and whatever else they may need. They will clean up and pay us $50.00 a Sunday rental. They want to start on Sunday, December 05. Do you have any problems or concerns with this? I assured him that Claire and I could work out any issues that may arise. I used this opportunity to advise him that the United Church was also in a similar financial predicament. The Reverend Joan White, their minister will probably approach you with a similar request. If asked, I think we should welcome them, as it would be a wonderful public sign of Christian unity.

He wanted to know if I had talked to my new house guest Father Raj yet? Yes, we talked well past my normal bedtime and had breakfast together. He is very companionable. The Bishop stated that the two of them had gone to Raj's parish for Sunday mass and to meet with his parishioners about the future of the parish. Raj has rented the school gym for this mass and for the meeting. We will have a lot to say about this at our next Deanery meeting. The Bishop said that he is thinking of assigning Father Raj to Father Ryan's Parish.

As I left his office, he said that he has come to rely on my counsel and he hopes that I will not get too busy to meet with him when he needs to consult and get a second opinion. He continued that he does not always agree with my suggestions, but wants to hear them regardless. I assured him that he could call me anytime.

As I left the Bishop's office, the thought crossed my mind that Ed would love to pass this juicy news to the Cardinal. Note to self: research the Church's position on both casinos and lotteries. I will ask Ed to assist me in this venture.

## Saturday Lunch with my Family

I had lunch with my parents as my father was not feeling well. Mother's home-made chicken noodle soup and fresh bread improved his condition. Under a promise of secrecy, even with my brother and sister, I confided that Bishop Ben has recommended me as someone with potential to become a Bishop. I have tried to discourage this action but I was not successful. They beamed with pride. I also told them about my new boarder Father Raj and his devastating church fire. They said that I should bring him to Sunday dinner. Before I left, they showed me their daily newspaper headline, "Catholic priest accused of sexually molesting two young boys." As I gave them a kiss on the cheek and a hug, I replied that I am still too shocked to talk to them about this now and that I would see them for dinner Sunday evening.

## Saturday/Sunday Masses (November 07/08): Preached Benedictine Spirituality

Mantra for the Day:

"Blessed are the clean of heart, when your inside world, mind and heart is put right, then you can see God in the outside world"
(Gospel of Matthew, ch. 5, v. 8).

*Dear friends, thank you for coming to Mass today. Thank you for inviting our loving Father into your lives today. I want to chat with you about Benedictine stability. I had a three-day retreat with the Benedictines this past week and now fell spiritually refreshed.*

*Monks live quiet regimented lives comprised of daily prayer, working on their farm, selling their produce and hospitality. I, however, want to focus today on the meaning of the vow of stability. Stability or enclosure in a monastic setting, means the acceptance of this particular community, this place and these monks, as the best way to live and to walk with God. Enclosure in spite of its negative connotation, is not considered a prison or a constraint on one's freedom. This spirituality of the monks is derived from the practice of the Rule by St. Benedict written some 1500 years ago and is based on the conviction that the rule speaks to those seeking God in the midst of a busy, frequently complex and sometimes exhausting daily life. Monks live lives that are very routine and predictable much like your lives are. When a monk starts experiencing thoughts of escaping, he knows he is tired of facing himself and his all too familiar personal struggles. I am reminded of an excerpt of a text from an early desert monk. A certain brother went to his Abbot asking him for advice on the path to holiness. The Abbot replied, "Go, sit in your cell and your cell will teach you everything."*

*What does this mean for you and me? A man or woman who voluntarily limits himself or herself to their same marital partner for the rest of their lives is saying that happiness and contentment is to be found with this particular partner and with no other. We are reminded that marriage and family life are a wonderful school of learning to love.*

*Stability can be very challenging given the changing situations to which we are subject, for example, the aging process, changes in employment or when sickness enters our family. In these situations, stability means persevering with patience or even to accepting personal hardship and suffering while this process evolves. It is allowing one's partner the freedom to work through these challenges. The family unit can acknowledge and be supportive of these inner emotional and spiritual journeys. God, our Father who loves us, will journeys with us.*

## Sunday dinner with family 5:00 PM

Father Raj asked me to thank my parents for the dinner invitation but he had been invited to spend the evening with the Bishop. He asked for a rain check. I, uncomfortably, was the centre of the discussion at the family dinner. Everyone, especially my siblings and their spouses, wanted my thoughts on who the priest was who was charged with sexually abusing the two boys, how serious were the charges, was there ample evidence and where was he? With the four children sequestered off into the family room in the basement with electronic games, I tried to share what I knew. First of all, in Canadian law, one is presumed innocent until found guilty by our peers. There is a hearing on Tuesday that will determine if the evidence is sufficient to go to trial and if bail is to be allowed. I prefer not to disclose the name of the priest until the papers do so on Wednesday. Bishop Ben and I are sick about it. More questions: how are the boys and how are the families? What is happening to them? Bishop Ben has met both families in their homes and has apologized. He has further recommended the two families to contact a family counselling agency where the costs will be borne by the Diocese. That is all I can say. Sis then inquired if this has ever happened before? She continued that she hoped that the Bishop would publicly release the name of this priest if he is found guilty and the names of former pedophiles if children and families were to be protected. While I understood their concern, I found their questions too intrusive and excused myself before dessert was served.

## Sunday evening 8:00 PM

Returning to the rectory, I phoned Sergeant Walker and explained our problem with Father Ryan. We need a safe secure place for our priest accused of pedophilia for the short term until his guilt or innocence is determined. He promised to look into it for me.

Father Raj arrived and we shared our shock and perspectives on the Ryan affair over rum and coke. He is a comforting presence and assured me that he loves to cook curries. This relationship might not last long, as the Bishop has asked Father Raj if he would replace Father Ryan in his parish during the trial until he can make other arrangements.

Father in heaven, I am feeling a little overwhelmed. I am suddenly reminded of all the neglect during my 20's to my family and especially to Wendy, my deceased wife, during her final days. My restorative time with the Benedictines feels like it occurred a year ago. Thank you for all the many seen and unseen things you do for my parishioners, my family and me. Protect Father Tim Ryan and help us find a safe place for him. Grant me the wisdom to navigate these stressful and challenging events without causing more pain.

## Monday, November 08
## Day off

Mantra for the Day:

"Remember that the Christian life is one of actions; not of words and daydreams. Let there be few words and many deeds, and let them be done well." St Vincent Pallotti (1795-1850)

I needed to write down my tasks for the next few weeks:

1. I need to get a photo of Father Tim Ryan for the Bishop; If judged guilty, we will need to send his name and photo in the National Registry of Pedophiles;
2. Talk to the town manager regarding the expansion plans for the town;
3. Talk to Bill McMillan and the men's group regarding the snow clearing of sidewalks and the management of rinks this winter;
4. Talk to parish council about our program for youth on clean water, affordable housing, soccer fields in a developing nation, preferably in Central America;
5. Get the marriage weekend plan going;
6. Get the Good Samaritan cooking course planned;
7. Remind Mabel and the Catholic Women's Association (CWA) to organize the girls and women's softball league; and,
8. Organize the temporary security in the parish for Father Ryan as a priority.

I phoned Father Joe, my favorite Benedictine, and explained the trouble we were having with Father Tim Ryan. He was very sympathetic. I approached him on whether his Order would consider taking on as a new type of work, the care of priests like the Father Ryans that are found guilty of pedophilia. I suspect every Bishop in North America has one or two of these tragic figures haunting them. According to all current research, there has been no success in their rehabilitation. I explained that our national penitentiary system abuses sex offenders. They need a safe place to face themselves and all the pain that they have caused. Bishop Ben is worried that Father Ryan will commit suicide and he does not want a Judas on his hands. He thanked me for thinking of them and assured me that he would present this to the Abbot. I said that please let me know if the Abbot would like to explore this idea further and I will get Bishop Ben to call him as well.

Father in heaven, thank you for another good day in your service. Protect the Pope, the Bishops, MP's and MLA's, the politicians who run our country, the police, the firemen and women, doctors, nurses, cleaning staffs and essential workers. Keep them in your love. A special prayer of thanks for Father Joe and the Benedictines.

## Tuesday, November 09
## Scripture study: The Gospel of Matthew

Mantra for the Day:

"You shall love the Lord, your God, with all your heart, with all your soul, and with all your mind. This is the greatest and the first commandment. The second is like it. You shall love your neighbour as yourself" (Gospel of Matthew, ch. 22, v. 37-39).

## Summary points:

1. The Gospel of Matthew holds a special place in Christianity as it is the first book of the New Testament.
2. The early Church erroneously thought that it had been the first Gospel written, whereas it was the Gospel of Mark.
3. The composer of Matthew's Gospel copied extensively from the Gospel of Mark.
4. This Gospel was the most utilized in worship in the early Church.
5. This Gospel contains some of the best loved passages in the New Testament as well as some of the most difficult teachings of Jesus.

6. The writer of this Gospel nowhere identifies himself and most scholars agree that it was not Matthew the tax collector.
7. The writer was likely a Jewish Christian, writing primarily for a community of Jewish Christians.
8. It was probably written around 85 CE, that would allow for the writing of the Gospel of Mark composed around 70 CE.
9. The locale for the religious community that he is writing to is thought to be Antioch in Syria, that had a large Jewish population and the centre of a growing Christianity community.

The core Christian beliefs as outlined in the Gospel of Matthew:

1. Matthew outlines the early years of Jesus, including the Visit of the Magi, the Flight to Egypt, Herod's slaughter of the children and His home in Nazareth.
2. The greatest commandment, "You shall love the Lord, your God with all your heart, with all your soul and with all your mind. This is the greatest and the first commandment. The second is like it: You shall love your neighbor as yourself."
3. Love your enemies, "You have heard that it was said, 'you shall love your neighbor and hate your enemy'. But I say to you, love your enemies and pray for those who persecute you, that you may be the children of your heavenly Father, for He makes His sun rise on the bad and the good, and causes the rain to fall on the just and the unjust."
4. Forgiveness and tolerance, "you have heard that it was said, 'an eye for an eye and a tooth for a tooth,' But I say to you, offer no resistance to one who is evil. When someone strikes you on your right cheek, offer your

left cheek as well. Should someone need you to carry something for a mile, go two miles. Give to the one who asks of you and do not turn your back on someone who is in need."
5. Judging others, "Stop judging that you may not be judged. For as you judge, so shall you be judged."
6. The final judgment will be determined on how well we cared for those less fortunate than us with food, clothing and the basics of life regardless of their worthiness. and
7. The passion, death and resurrection of Christ.

Late afternoon, Sergeant Walker phoned and left a message confirming that if the Diocese needed a safe secure place for Father Ryan, there were secure cells in both the RCMP quarters and the hospital that could be utilized in the short term. He or his colleague will be transporting Father Ryan to and from the Courthouse for his upcoming trial. He has discussed this with his superior officers and given the special circumstances, they have agreed accommodate him. He concurred that Father Ryan would not be safe in either a city jail or a provincial prison. As the RCMP do not have a cook preparing meals, the hospital will provide them. I still needed photos of Father Ryan for the local and the national papers in the event he was to be found guilty;

Father in heaven, thank you for the opportunity to study your word, reflect upon it and to absorb it into my bones. It is at times like this, that I wished there were Jewish community with whom I could study and pray. I would love to know their perspective. Someday, hopefully. Thank you for helping to arrange a safe place for Father Tim. I wonder what he must be going through. Please protect him.

# Wednesday, November 10
# Catching up on paperwork

Mantra for the day:

"When you pray, go into your inner room, close the door and pray to your heavenly Father in secret. And your Father who sees in secret, will repay you. In praying, do not use many words. Your Father knows what you need before you ask him" (Gospel of Matthew, ch. 6, v. 6-8).

The Bishop phoned me at 9:00 am with the news that Father Ryan had been denied bail and that the Court had determined that there was sufficient evidence for him to stand trial. The three-day trial has been scheduled to begin on Tuesday, November 23 at 10:00 am at the Provincial Court. It will be a trial by a judge alone, not a judge and jury. He has hired a very reputable lawyer, Paul Taylor to properly defend him. By the way, Paul is also a good Catholic.

I am glad that the Bishop was not going to throw Father Ryan under the bus, regardless of the level of difficulty he was in. He expressed his appreciation for my arranging a safe haven for Father Ryan. Would you and Father Raj please make a point to visit him and try to understand what has led him at sexually assault these two boys? We cannot abandon him in his hour of need. I am worried that he will commit suicide to deal with his regret, guilt and depression. He expressed his appreciation, a second time, for arranging a safe place for Father Ryan.

I phoned the Town Manager Todd Joseph, and told him that I would happily make my professional knowledge and experience in affordable housing available to town staff. I also told him that I am quite busy doing parish work. He thanked me for taking the initiative with the parishioners in assuming the park maintenance for the town. He asked if it would be more convenient with me if certain meetings that focussed on housing matters were held at my home? I wholeheartedly agreed. I also informed him about my friend Stanley Robinson, a retired town planner with whom I have worked. I suggested that his training and experience would be valuable to him and the town administration going forward. He agreed and took his contact information that I provided, thanking me warmly. I informed him that I would give Stanley a heads up that you might call him. He was very appreciative. That was easy.

I phoned Bill McMillan and left him a message on his phone asking if the men's group would take the leadership and the management of the park maintenance program in the summer and perhaps snow clearing in the winter. I also suggested that he could advertise through Ed's paper for men from the community to assist.

I emailed the Bishop asking his permission to organize a group of parish assistants comprised of couples who have demonstrated leadership qualities over the years. I foresee these couples doing pre-marriage counselling, sacramental preparation for first communion and confirmation, officiating at parish baptisms, weddings and funerals. I also see them leading liturgical services when a priest cannot be present and delivering a short homily or sermon. Examples include the three couples you met from the parish who attended the Deanery meeting in October. There are also new leaders coming forward expressing a desire to help the parish and the community. While they would be technically performing the duties of a deacon, I prefer to call them parish assistants to avoid any conflicts with the Vatican.

I also mentioned too that Colin and Marion, the couple that we encouraged to return to the Church, are a delightful gift. Colin phoned me to say Marion's former husband, was recently found dead on the streets in Vancouver from a drug overdose. City authorities found her contact information on his person and informed her of his death. Colin and Marion decided that he should be cremated in Vancouver and his cremains shipped here for burial where he could be given a proper and dignified burial. They wanted to know if they could have a funeral service in the parish and bury him in our cemetery? I said yes provided it remains a private ceremony both in the Church and at graveside. Then I thought, does anything remain private in this community? They quickly agreed and it is scheduled for next Saturday morning. (When we get around to reviewing the Church's teaching on divorce, Marion's care and concern for her former down and out husband compensates for any negativity about divorce, in my opinion.)

I need to ask Mabel to take the lead on our South American programs that include providing clean water, sports fields for soccer and baseball and affordable housing. She and the CWA can call on Claire Meadows (Anglican Church priest) and Joan White (United Church minister) for support;

I must phone Jerome to find out about the plans for the parish men's cooking course;

Note to self: I need to find some private time to organize the marriage renewal weekend. First item tomorrow morning.

Father in heaven, thank you the wonderful opportunities you give me. I have noticed in my quiet time with you that I eat whenever I get anxious instead of eating only when I am hungry. What does that mean? Then there is my love of wine. I drink a glass of wine at dinner. Am I becoming addicted? Thank you for your protection and love. Help me to be more regular spending my quiet time with you. Protect Father Ryan, Mabel, Bill, Jerome, Colin, Marion and their families and friends. Keep them close to your heart. Please be extra especially kind to Father Raj as he seems lost without his church and a home.

## Thursday, November 11
## Office work and Men's Group Meeting

Mantra for the Day:

"For the Lord is good; his steadfast love endures forever, and his faithfulness to all generations" (Book of Psalms, ch. 100, v. 5).

As it was Remembrance Day, we had a good crowd at mass this morning. After mass, Ned went to Tim Horton's and brought back coffee and donuts for breakfast. The talk over breakfast was on uncles and aunts who had fought and died in wars that Canadians had fought in.

The Bishop replied to my email requesting a detail plan on the training of the pastoral assistants before he would agree to the idea.

Jerome replied with some dates for the men's cooking course and requested a meeting to discuss if he and Raymond could be married at St. Francis. Why am I surprised?

1. Draft pastoral assistants training program for Bishop Ben,

    a) Purpose: to train adult men and women of the parish to lead small Eucharistic prayer services with general absolution, to provide the parish ministries of baptisms, marriage celebrations, counselling the sick, burials and marriage preparation courses with basic Church teachings based on a scripture-based information coupled with the Church's teaching on these sacraments;

    b) Marriage preparation course: I will be preparing a handout on Christian/Catholic marriage based on biblical stories of Adam and Eve, Abraham and Sara, Ruth and Boaz, Hosea and Jesus' teaching on marriage. Addition to the handout, I will be suggesting a one-hour sessions with a perspective couple to cover a) the basic requirement of being free to marry and to have the basic knowledge of expectations in marriage, b) a one-hour session with a medical doctor on sexuality (male and female sexual responses) with a medically recommended text book and Q and A's with a medical doctor, c) the Catholic view of Christian love and d) the role of forgiveness and non-judgmental behaviors in a person's emotional and spiritual development;

c) Selection: the parish through its organizations will nominate the candidates;

d) When: this program will begin in January, meet once a week for two hours, one hour of Scripture training using my class notes and one hour of practice. Once the training period is completed, the group will become a support group where practice of homilies, the refining of pre-marriage instructions through the raising of questions and concerns. I expect that the training of this group will extend for four months and be ready to practice in April, next year. Through this process, it is my hope that this group will train others as the need arises.

e) Completion of the eight-week course: I am hopeful that Bishop Ben will preside over this celebration.

## Men's Group meeting at 7:00 pm:

Attendance was small with only four men present: Bill, Fred, Colin and Ned. Before all the questions started, I advised them that Father Raj Patel from St. Thomas Parish will be living with me temporarily. His church and rectory burned to the ground Monday last week. Of course, the conversation then went immediately on Father Ryan. They wanted all the details but more importantly why, why, why? I agreed that this was deeply shocking. I further explained that he has only been charged and not convicted by a court of law. He goes to trial on November 23. Due the potential harm that inmates do to suspected or convicted pedophiles, he will remain in custody in our hospital secured room during the trial. The concern is finding him a safe long-term place for him if he is found guilty. The Bishop is concerned about his mental health. Therefore, he has requested that Father Raj and I visit him at the hospital regularly. It would be a wonderful gesture if some of you could do that too. He will not be a danger for you.

They expressed shocked that a priest, a man of God, could do such horrific acts. Could the Bishop ever trust him again doing parish work? Even if he is found to be innocent, could the Bishop trust him with other work? They acknowledged that the Courts seem to provide very generous compensations to the victims and their families and could the Diocese afford a large court ordered restitution-order?

Once they had voiced their shock, disappointment, and anger, the meeting ground down to a halt. Bill acknowledged my phone call and alerted the others of our desire to contribute to the community with summer grace-cutting, park clean-up, winter rink maintenance and snow-shovelling programs. We would also pay some unemployed to help too. Ed would be asked to put notices in our local newspaper.

I informed the men's group that Bishop Ben had agreed to allow the Anglicans to rent our Church for weekly services. They will begin on December 05 with a potluck dinner in the parish hall at 5:00 pm and a Liturgy at 6:00 pm. They expect to be completed at 7:30 pm. These guys were intrigued as Catholics were raised to fast from food before going to Mass. They suggested that a notice should be placed in the parish bulletin. I agreed.

I asked the men how many had planned on attending the men's cooking course? Twelve spots were the maximum number allowed. They suspected that men from the community would be interested if allowed.

Bill then asked me to recommend a practice to help him deal with his sexual thoughts about other women? He began, "Do you and your priest colleagues have sexual thoughts about women?"

How did we get into this issue? I replied, "Yes, most men generally do and so do I; having been married and having enjoyed a short but active sex life, that is now part of my personal DNA. I told them about an old friend of mine, a senior citizen, who told me that even in his 80's, he still finds women sexually attractive. For me, memories of Wendy relate more to my regrets and grief about not having done enough for her when she was dying. But to answer your question; men and women are complementary and there are strong biological and emotional bonds between us. I have met women of varying ages who are stunningly beautiful. My problem with sexual fantasies is worse when I go to bed at night after a long day, but I have found reciting the Lord's prayer helps me to quickly fall sleep. This prayer is like a tranquillizer for me."

Bill continued, "What about sexual thoughts about a woman other than your wife?"

I suggested that this was normal for men. It probably is not a problem unless you start acting on it. If it begins to interfere with your marriage, you should see a marriage counselor or a therapist.

Fred asked if this conversation could remain confidential. I assured him that for me it was. The others quickly agreed.

## Late night chai tea with Father Raj

Father Raj and I had chai after my meeting. He commented on how great Bishop Ben was with his parishioners. He just listened to their sadness and disappointment in the loss of their Church and rectory. He asked them if they would agree to celebrating weekday masses either in a vacant commercial or industrial space while they waited the results of the cause of the fire and began to plan for the future. He explained that Father Raj would be residing in Father Ryan's former parish and temporarily managing two parishes. So, continue to keep connected with Father Raj by either telephone or internet.

I informed Father Raj that the Anglicans in the community would be renting our Church for the foreseeable future. I explained all the details to him. It gave him much to think about. He thanked me for my generous hospitality.

Father in heaven, thank you for another wonderful day serving you and the people of St Francis. Keep Father Raj and the men of the parish in your loving care.

## Friday, November 12
## Office Work

Mantra for the Day:

"It is the Lord who keeps faith forever, who executes justice for the oppressed and who gives food to the hungry. The Lord sets the prisoners free" (Book of Psalms, ch. 146, v. 6-7).

Mother phoned me shortly after 9:00 am wondering how I am handling all the stress about that "poor" priest, Father Ryan. I assured her that I was doing fine. She also wanted to know how my freezer was? Was there still enough food for you and your guests? I assured her again that my guests love her cooking but they also love Mario's fine Italian take-out. I asked her when she would like to come out for an overnight. She said as soon as your father is back on his feet.

I phoned Stanley Robinson, the retired city planner, explaining to him the nature of the proposed developments in our community. Would he consider working with the Town Council and the Town Administration to provide them with professional planning advice during this process. I assured him that they could use his calm professional experience. He agreed and I terminated our call by stating that Todd Joseph, the Town Manager would call him shortly.

I phoned Todd informing him of my conversation with Stanley. He agreed immediately follow up with a phone call to him. He thanked me profusely.

Father in heaven, thank you again for another good day in your service. It was wonderful hearing from my mother, Stanley Robinson and Todd Joseph. I hope that they can work well together.

## Saturday/Sunday, November 13/14
## Preach the Gospel of Matthew

Mantra for the Day:

"When you pray, go to your inner room, close the door, and pray to your Father in secret. And you Father who sees in secret will repay you" (Gospel of Matthew, ch. 6, v. 6).

*"My dear friends, my homily today is on St. Matthew's Gospel. But I would like to preface my remarks by telling you about an encounter I had this week. I was walking to a meeting with the*

*Bishop and was approached by what appeared to me as a homeless man, asking for money. He was close enough for me to smell alcohol on his breath. I offered to take him to a nearby Tim Horton's for food. Once inside, he couldn't make up his mind on what he wanted. So, I asked him if he would like the money instead? He sheepishly looked down and whispered yes. I suspected that he would use the money to buy some rubbing alcohol to drink. I reluctantly gave him the money knowing that I was enabling him to continue drinking. Enabling or giving them money in these situations is severely frowned upon by those in the alcoholic treatment business.*

*Upon reflection, was I being judgemental, arrogant and opinionated? Yes. How would I know what his real needs were? I was reminded by Christ's teaching in the Gospel of Matthew that we are supposed to see Christ in the homeless, the hungry and the sick and to care for them. No questions asked. How foolish to think that we can control how a gift we give, can be used.*

*The Gospel of Matthew is a special treat for someone like me who has studied social work. Matthew added that being non-judgemental was essential in our relationships with others. Being non-judgmental is a basic tenet of social work practice. In addition, he stated that heaven required that we care for the sick, the homeless and the vulnerable. Basic social work practice.*

*But the Gospel of Matthew is also about love. Not only are we supposed to love our Father in heaven, but love and serve our neighbour. If someone however, offended us, we were to avoid retaliation but instead we were to turn the other cheek. How easy is that? If someone asks for help, we are to respond with more than we were asked for.*

*At the end of the day, our Christian practice is doing the best we can. While imperfect, we strive to treat others justly, to be kind and to walk humbly with our Father in heaven."*

## Sunday dinner with the family: 5:00 pm

Dinner with the family was very pleasant; no discussion on Father Ryan. It was as if they agreed beforehand not to raise this uncomfortable subject with me. The focus of the debate was considering having a family Christmas in a warmer climate such as Arizona or California. My sister and brother are encouraging my parents to go south for a few months to avoid the harsh winters. I had nothing to say but enjoyed the four nieces and nephews' excited reactions to a possible side trip to Disneyland. When Sis asked me for my opinion, I told her that Christmas and Easter were my busiest times of the year. I however, could join them for a few days after Christmas. My new house-mate, Father Raj could take over in my absence.

## Tea with Father Raj

I am slowly developing a taste for chai tea. Raj does not drink anything else. I wonder what my inner health would be like if I were to stop drinking four cups of strong coffee a day. Raj had a wonderful weekend with the Bishop and Max.

Thank you, Father, for all that you do for me, keeping me safe from delusions of grandeur. Thank you for my parishioners, Father Raj, my family, for Bishop Ben (and Max of course), my fellow priests and those who search for answers.

## Monday, November 15
## Day off,

> Mantra for the Day:
>
> "The Lord supports the orphan and the widow but the way of the wicked, he brings to ruin" (Book of Psalms, ch. 146, v. 9).

Thank you, Father for a catch-up day. I was able to do some preparatory work on tomorrow's scripture class on St. John's gospel, update my task list, do some laundry, visit Father Ryan. My visit with him was very brief as he refused to talk to me. He would not even look at me. But he looked comfortable in his cell. He has a small TV, books, a desk, a bed, a toilet and a window. He is eating well but is very incommunicative. I emailed the Bishop outlining all this. The Bishop responded by saying that the Wednesday scheduled deanery meeting would be held in his office beginning at 10:00 am.

## Tuesday, November 16
## Scripture Study, the Gospel of John

> Mantra for the Day:
>
> "Whoever loves me will keep my word, and my Father will love them, and we will come to them and make our home in them"
> (Gospel of John, ch. 14, v. 23).

# Summary notes of my class on the Gospel and the Letters of John

Introduction:

- In the Gospels of Matthew, Mark and Luke, Jesus is portrayed as a human person whereas in the Gospel of John, he is portrayed as serene, above the fray and in total control of his life and his destiny on earth.
- Unique to John, the Gospel has only seven miracles and no exorcisms. The raising of Lazarus is unique to John.
- While the Gospel is attributed to John the apostle, the author is unknown.
- The Gospel of John has a very dualistic view of the world; things are black and white, light and darkness, spirit and flesh.
- The Gospel of John was written around 90 CE while the early Christian community was experiencing acrimonious experiences with fellow Jews.
- The Letters of John were written around 100 – 115 CE and probably by the same author.
- The First Letter uses the style of a homily, whereas the Second and Third Letters can be characterized as using a letter format.

Central teachings:

1) Just as God, our loving Father revealed Himself through the various books of the Old Testament, now our loving Father reveals himself in his son, Jesus of Nazareth. To know Jesus, is to know our loving God.
2) Jesus is the ultimate example of our loving God's self-sacrificing gift to us.
3) It is dying on the cross that Jesus manifests his love and obedience to the Father.

4) "Let us love one another, because love is from God. Everyone who loves, is born of God and experiences a relationship with God."
5) "God is love, and whoever remains in love, remains in God and God in him."
6) Jesus' mission on earth was to reveal the Father. This is our mission too. We are to reveal both the Father and the Son within us, by our love and service of those around us.
7) The Gospel reflects John's community that includes Israelites, followers of John the Baptist, Jewish people cured by Jesus, Greeks, Samaritans who emphasize discipleship and the presence of the Holy Spirit.
8) The early Christians live in an uneasy relationship with the unbelieving world comprised of Pharisees who reject Jesus, Christians whose beliefs are minimalistic and those who practice their Christianity in secret.

Father in heaven, thank you for the review of John's teachings. They are an important reminder of the importance of loving. As always, I ask you to love and protect the Pope, the Bishops, my family, my parishioners, the homeless, the sick and those who have no hope.

## Wednesday, November 17
## Priest's Deanery meeting,

Mantra for the Day:

"I give you a new commandment: love one another. As I have loved you, so you should love one another. This is how all will know that you are my disciples, if you have love for one another" (Gospel of John, ch. 13, v. 34-35).

The Bishop opened the meeting. Max made his usual rounds for rubs and hugs; calming everyone down with his sympathetic eyes. Our regular group were in attendance along with Father Mike. The Bishop updated everyone on Father Ryan and when he finished, he asked me for my observations of him. I reported that I had visited him. While he refused to talk to me, he is well cared for as he waits his trial. His behavior could imply that he is very depressed, worried and remorseful.

The Bishop explained that while Father Ryan has a good lawyer representing him, the trial and the trauma to the two families will cost the Diocese a considerable sum of money that they do not have. The boys and their families may need long term counselling and are entitled to financial compensation. Court charges are not cheap. Father Cam has suggested that the Diocese run a lottery to make extra money. Houses are frequently used as prizes for lotteries. This is still under advisement.

Next the fire that destroyed Father Raj's St. Thomas' Church and rectory was discussed. The future of a new church and/or its closure is still under discussion. Father Raj will assume responsibility for Father Ryan's parish. In In the meantime, he asked for a report from each of us outlining the financial status of your church and rectory, the maintenance plans and insurance carried. He also wanted us to suggest fund raising options. He closed by saying that Father Raj would be celebrating mass with his St. Thomas parishioners in the United Church on Saturdays and in St. George's on Sundays replacing Father Ryan and would be temporarily residing with Father Mike.

Father in heaven, thank you for this day. Thank you for allowing me to work with you, the Bishop and my fellow priests. I have begun to notice my impatience, a problem that Wendy used to remind me about. My weak computer skills annoy me greatly. I have had to phone my computer specialist a number of times recently and sometimes he seems very slow in returning my calls. I wonder if this means that I am in danger of returning to my old work-alcoholic ways. Christ was also impatient with the apostles, the money changers in the temple and the Pharisees. Why would I not have such a personal problem? Thank you, Father for this awareness. Take care of those that I serve.

## Thursday, November 18
## Meeting with my Interdenominational Colleagues,

>Mantra for the Day:
>
>"Come to me, all you that are weary and heavy-burdened and I will give you rest." (Gospel of Matthew, ch. 11, v. 28).

Our usual group were in attendance: Claire Meadows (Anglican Church), Joan White (United Church), Don Keating (Lay Buddhist practitioner), Peter Smith (Just curious) and Ed Malone (Editor, Prairie News). This group is like no other and their light-hearted chatter reflected that. I wonder what they think of my shadow.

After a short introductory prayer, Claire asked for the floor. She excitedly announced that her parish would be closing and it would be renting space from St. Francis. She explained that their numbers were down they could not afford to maintain their church. The Anglican Bishop has already secured a potential purchaser but they are not prepared to release the name yet. Bishop Ben has been a champion for them. They will start their new tenure on Sunday, December 05, with a potluck a dinner at 5:00 pm followed by the celebration of their liturgy at 6:00 pm. All are welcome but please bring a dish or two. She asked Ed to put a notice in his weekly newspaper to spread the word. Joan inquired if her United Church congregation could also join this union if needed. Her parish was also struggling financially and with a declining membership. I assured her that I would never under any circumstances turn her and her congregation away. Joan asked if her parishioners could receive the Eucharist? I stated that anyone who believed that Jesus was present in the Eucharist, was welcome to receive the Eucharist. Ed asked about amalgamating all three churches in the community. He thought that if all the churches used one place of worship, it would be such a good example for the community. (I had better alert Bishop Ben of the United Church wanting to rent space from St. Francis and that he should alert the Cardinal to avoid him being blind-sided by this news from Ed).

## Catholics 1   Protestants 0

I updated them on the Father Ryan affair and they did not have too much to say, thank goodness. Probably because of the sensitivity of the subject. Joan asked for the floor and asked if the Catholic Church would ever allow women priests? While not knowing a priest personally except for me, she wondered if the practice of living and working alone can turn them into being self-centred like anyone can who lives alone? She expressed a lot of sympathy for Father Ryan. Could his actions, while very abhorrent, be considered a cry out for help? I thanked Joan for her kind and perceptive thoughts but did not have a good response to her inquiry. In response to your original question, I explained that there are validly ordained women priests approximately 145 of them actively working in small groups of Catholics and their friends. They are not recognized by the official Church in Rome. To complicate things even more, Pope Benedict, the former Pope, has allowed Anglican male priests with wives and children to join the Catholic Church and function as married priests. Claire jumped in asking what was the Catholic Church's problem with women? She wondered if the Catholic Church would have fewer sexual problems if there were married male and female priests. Ed then asked about the possibility of gay male and female priests? Would it not make sense to have gay male and female priests to better understand and care for this growing population? It sounds like a no brainer? (The Cardinal would love to be a fly on the wall at this meeting.)

## Catholics 1    Protestants 2

Then Ed led a discussion on the significance of the chicken processing plant coming to the community and the community eventually doubling in size. He then pointed at me saying that we have our very own house building expert as Father Cam has had years of experience in land development before he became a priest. We also talked about the two community service programs; the snow shovelling in the winter and the grass cutting of parks in the summers. I informed them that Bill McMillan, one of our parishioners was spearheading this project. Ed jumped in saying that Bill has already contacted him requesting to announce it in our weekend paper and advertising for workers.

Ed said that some of the members of the community had seen me wondering around in the ditches at the entrance to the town. "Were you lost or troubled?"

"No", I replied, "Just taking my turn picking up garbage and litter." To provide a context for my actions, I then told them the story of Zhou En-lai (1898-1976), the former Premier of the People's Republic of China who regularly took his turn cleaning the streets. I remember seeing photos of him with a long broom sweeping the garbage in the streets. We all need to contribute.

## Catholics 2   Protestants 2

Don Keating asked if he could open a discussion on the problems that Christians have on dualistic thinking. He continued, "Christians spend a lot of time dealing with duality. For example, they turn life into good and evil, black and white, light and darkness, you and me, we and Mother Earth." He is studying world religions in an on-line course and in particular Buddhism. He finds that the Eastern religions and the religious practices of our Indigenous people avoid dualistic thinking.

"They believe that everything is inter-connected and all things are on a continuum. With the result that we when hurt someone, even unknowingly, we diminish ourselves. When we pollute the environment, we pollute ourselves." (Note to self: I need to have coffee with Don and learn more about this.).

## Catholics 2   Protestants 2   Buddhists 1

Claire asked if they could put up a creche or Christmas stable scene in the Church, if we were not going to do one. I thanked her but asked her to give me a few days to see if the parish had one.

## Catholics 2   Buddhists 1   Protestants 3

Peter inquired about a Christmas dinner for the community that would cater to low income people and their families. It could provide a small gift like a book for all the children. Books would encourage reading. Ed suggested using casino monies to pay for it. Claire suggested the high school gym. Ed could advertise it in his newspaper. Claire and Joan agreed to lead in the organization of this event. Ed would start advertising it in his weekend newspaper and would request that interested families and individuals to contact Claire (697-454-3345) or Joan (697- 555-6677). We agreed to meet again in two weeks

## Catholics 2   Buddhists 1   Protestants 4

Father in heaven, Ed is going to have a field day of newsworthy items for his newspaper and for his friend the Cardinal. As usual, loving Father, I pray for the Pope, the Bishops, my priest colleagues, Father Ryan, my parishioners, my family especially my parents as they age, the sick, the lonely, the homeless. Keep them all in your love and protection.

## Friday, November 19
## Catch Up Day

Mantra for the Day:

"The Lord is gracious and merciful, slow to anger and consistent in steadfast love. The Lord is good to all and his compassion is over all that he has made" (Book of Psalms, ch. 145, v. 8-9).

- Don has agreed to a morning coffee next Wednesday.
- I emailed the Bishop and outlined the content of our meeting with my Protestant colleagues, explaining in some detail Claire's exuberance about the Anglicans moving into our parish church and perhaps even Joan's United Church. I also reminded him that Ed Malone was in attendance and that can mean that the Cardinal will hear about this tomorrow.
- The Bishop replied that while he appreciated the heads up, he was dealing with more challenging problems. He mentioned in passing that the Benedictines were pleased to be offered to take on a new role of caring

for sexual offenders (not just priests). He and the Abbot were meeting with the Cardinal next week in Toronto with representatives of the Federal Penitentiary Service to further flesh out the financial details. In the meantime, if Father Ryan is found guilty, the Bishop will request that the Court assign him to the monastery with an ankle bracelet until a more secured facility is constructed.

Father in heaven, thank you for all that You do for me.

## Saturday/Sunday, November 20/21
## Preach the Gospel of John

Mantra for the Day:

"If we love one another, God will live in us in perfect love" (First Letter of John, ch. 4, v. 12).

*"Dear friends, thank you for coming to Mass. Today, I want to chat with you about the Gospel of John. In our scripture course last Tuesday, we spent most of the day studying the unique elements of this gospel and the letters. It is safe to conclude that John the apostle did not write this book and the letters, but someone who knew him well. The Gospel of John was written around 90 CE while the early Christian community was experiencing acrimonious experiences with fellow Jews.*

*While in the Gospels of Matthew, Mark and Luke, Jesus is portrayed as a human person, in the Gospel of John however, he is portrayed as serene, above the fray and in total control of his life and his destiny on earth. Just as our loving*

*God, the Father revealed Himself through the various books of the Old Testament, now our loving Father reveals himself in his son, Jesus of Nazareth. To know Jesus, is to know our loving God. Jesus is the ultimate example of our loving God's self-sacrificing gift to us; In his dying on the cross, Jesus manifests his love and obedience to the Father.*

*John's Gospel is also known as the Gospel of love. 'Let us love one another, because love is from God. Everyone who loves, is born of God and experiences a relationship with God.' These words alone justify treating our non-Catholic brothers and sisters with love and respect. Where we encounter loving and kind behavior, we are encountering God. John again teaches that 'God is love, and whoever remains in love, remains in God and God in him'.*

*The Gospel reflects John's community that includes Israelites, followers of John the Baptist, Jewish people cured by Jesus, Greeks, Samaritans who emphasize discipleship and the presence of the Holy Spirit. The early Christians live in an uneasy relationship with the unbelieving world comprised of Pharisees who reject Jesus, Christians whose beliefs are minimalistic and those who practice their Christianity in secret.*

*Jesus' mission on earth was to reveal His loving Father. This is our mission too. We are to reveal both the Father and the Son and the Holy Spirit living within us, by our love and service of those around us."*

## Sunday Dinner with family

The big news was that the family has rented a house in San Diego for January. It has four bedrooms and three bathrooms. My parents will spend the month there and my brother and sister will each have two weeks with five days when all three families will be there together. They wanted to know when I could join. I assured them that I would join them when I could and for as long as I could. I would not miss it for the world.

My good news about the Anglicans renting space at St. Francis drew blank looks. Mother was the only one who expressed her pleasure in my news.

Father Raj sent me an email asking if he can come by tomorrow for coffee. I assured him yes.

Father in heaven, thank you for a wonderful day in your service. Thank you for my family who help to keep my ego under control.

## Monday, November 22
## Day off,

Mantra for the Day:

"Let us love one another, because love is from God; the love we have for others is a gift from God" (First letter of John, ch 4, v. 7)

Father Raj arrived on time at 10:00 am. With a cup of chai tea in hand, he began by explaining to me that he had spent three weeks in June last year visiting family, friends and colleagues in India. He unexpectedly met an old female friend, Masala from high school. They last talked thirty years ago. Masala is now a tenured professor; her subject is the history of India. She never married to the disappointment of her family;

too independent and academic for Indian men and finds the patriarchal norms of Indian society quite disturbing. She is now considered an outsider and wants to leave India. They felt an immediate connection. Raj encouraged her to move to Canada. Lo and behold, she is now teaching at a university in Western Canada. They have been corresponding both by letter and on the internet. He thinks that he may be in love with her and senses her feelings for him might be mutual. The issue is compounded by his heavy work load. The Bishop has him working in two parishes, celebrating mass on Saturday in St. Thomas and driving to St. George's for Sunday mass. He went on that he feels so much better as a person with her in his life. What should he do? He is 45 years of age. Should he talk about this with the Bishop?

I replied that he was lucky to have a special woman in his life. I advised him that my life with Wendy, albeit short-lived, has certainly influenced my priestly work for the better. I recommended that he pray hard to find out what our loving Father's will was for him. Be honest and candid with Masala. Let's have lunch in a couple of weeks in the City. I would suggest too that you consult my Benedictine friend, Father Joe. He is a very wise old soul. I would also consult a professional psychologist to help you understand what is happening to you. Whatever you decide to do, I will support you and assist you in any way that I can. We had more tea and he was gone. I thanked him kindly for sharing his story with me.

Jerome emailed me to ask if Mondays, Wednesdays or Fridays evenings for the men's cooking course would work for me. I replied yes to Wednesday. He said that the hospital had agreed to their use of the kitchen from 7:00 to 10:00 pm. The class would be a hands-on class but only for a small group as the kitchen is not that large. Do you know how many men will attend the three-evening course? Could you please confirm the number by this Friday?

I apologized for not getting back to him on an appointment for he and Raymond. I said that we could meet after the Good Samaritan meeting scheduled for Friday at 7:30 pm or Saturday morning at 10:00 am. He immediately emailed me with the following dates: November 22, 29 and December 06 for the cooking classes.

Father in heaven, thank you for Father Raj, Masala, Jerome, Raymond and their friends. Keep them close to You.

# Tuesday, November 23
# Scripture Study, the Gospel of Luke

Mantra for the Day

"The Pharisees and their religious scholars came to his disciples greatly offended. 'What is he (Jesus) doing eating and drinking with misfits and 'sinners'?' Jesus heard about it and spoke up, 'Who needs a doctor: the healthy or the sick? I'm here inviting outsiders, not insiders; an invitation to a changed life, changed inside and out" (Gospel of Luke, ch. 5, v. 30-32).

## Summary of class notes:

1. The Gospel of Luke is the first part of a two-part history of early Christianity. The first part is the Gospel of Luke that begins with the birth of Christ and ends with His ascension into heaven. The second part is the Acts of the Apostles that outlines the story of the early Church from Christ's ascension (around 33 CE) to Paul's death in Rome (around 62 CE).

2. Dante called Luke's Gospel "the scribe of Christ's gentleness" because of his focus on Jesus' mercy to sinners and the outcasts of society. Luke includes the stories of Jesus' mercy to the widow of Naim (who was not Jewish), the prodigal son (who asked for his inheritance early, spent it riotously and was welcomed back in the family by his father) and Zacchaeus (a hated tax collector who worked for the Romans).
3. Luke was a Greek-speaking Christian, writing in Antioch (in what is today Turkey) between 80 and 90 CE.
4. The Christian Church had become more Gentile than Jewish in composition; moved from Jerusalem and as spreading throughout the Roman Empire.
5. Whereas Matthew wrote for the Jewish community, Luke shows the connectivity of the early Gentile Church to Jesus. He uses the existing Gospel of Mark (66-74 CE) and other sources used in the Gospel of Matthew (80-90 CE) to explain Jesus to a non-Jewish world.
6. These new Christians of Asia Minor and Europe wanted to be good citizens of the Roman Empire. They were well-to-do and more urban than rural. They wanted to know how Jesus' words to the Jewish people a long time ago could be relevant for their time.
7. Luke's unique themes are:

   a) A loving relationship with a loving God is available to everyone:

   God loves all of us, his creatures and wants to be in relationship with each of us now and in our afterlife.

   b) Mercy and forgiveness:

   Luke presents to us an image of God as Father who is constantly seeking those who are lost. In

Chapter 15, there are three special parables; the lost sheep, the lost coin and the prodigal son. In the latter example, the father leaves his home to meet his repentant son and then to reassure his older son, the jealous brother, that his inheritance is intact. God portrayed as a loving and forgiving father.

c) Concern for women and disadvantages groups.

Jesus as very concerned about women who were second class citizens, frequently the poor and the outcasts. Poor shepherds instead of educated wise Magi, welcomed Jesus into this world. Jesus welcomes a sinful but penitent woman at a Pharisee's meal. Jesus spoke well of Samaritans who were considered outcastes because they had inter-married with non-Jewish neighbours. Jesus seeks the hospitality of Zacchaeus, a wealthy tax collector supervisor who was suspected of cheating not only his tax collector employees but also ordinary people on tax money collected for the Romans. Jesus befriends women who were often mistreated at that time with the result that they stood with him during his passion and kept watch at his death on the cross.

d) Joy:

This Gospel consistently expresses the joy of being connected with Jesus. There are many examples of Jesus expressing his love and mercy to all. The births of Jesus and John the Baptist are explained as occasions of great joy. The return of an outsider or someone who was lost, is a source of great joy in heaven.

e) The Holy Spirit:

This Gospel emphasizes the role of the Holy Spirit. The Holy Spirit is involved in Jesus' birth, leads Jesus into the desert and empowers the disciples to preach the Gospel.

f) Prayer:

Prayer is a significant part of Jesus' life on earth

g) Modern Christian living:

This Gospel makes the teachings of Jesus applicable to his middle-class readers. Being a good Roman citizen is compatible with Christianity.

The Bishop emailed me to say that he has sat through the three days of testimony of Father Ryan's Court case. The Judge has adjourned the trial and will deliver his verdict in three weeks, December 09. Father Ryan looks miserable. He had cautioned Paul Taylor, the lawyer, not to make the objective of this case to reduce the compensation or the need of counselling for the victims of these horrible events. All the Bishop wanted was for Father Ryan to receive a fair trial.

Father in heaven, thank you for the Gospel of Luke.

# Wednesday, November 24
# Meeting with Don and the CWA meeting,

Mantra for the Day:

"God is love and whoever remains in love, remains in God and God in him" (First Letter of John, ch. 4, v. 16).

Don came by for coffee. He brought blueberry bran muffins. Another weakness of mine. If I don't get control of my eating habits, I will be weighing three hundred pounds before long. He is so polite; he thanked me for my taking time from my busy life to sit with him as he was neither a Catholic nor a member of the St. Francis Parish. He jumped right into our previous discussion about dualistic thinking. The problem, you Catholics have, he continued is with dualistic thinking for example, good and bad, white and black, yin and yang. In Buddhism, there are no opposites and all of life is inter-connected. As he had said in the meeting, loving someone enhances them and makes you feel better. Hurting them hurts yourself. The Asian culture is far more conscious of this connectivity. This is particularly true with the environment. Your Pope Francis, a big environmentalist has written extensively on the need to protect the environment particularly for the vulnerable people living in developing nations. We are connected to nature in all its forms. From my studies on Christianity, he went on, Christ taught that whatever we did to the most insignificant, we did to him. Over fishing or over harvesting of the fish stocks can affect our lifestyle. Think of indigenous peoples. They clearly have no concept of land ownership in their culture. They are only the managers of the land for the future generations. If Christians really believe that God created the world and all the creatures in it, how can you justify ownership or control of it for yourselves? Ownership can result in dualistic view of the world; them and us, rich and poor. Ownership can lead to feelings of entitlement.

He controlled the conversation while I made more coffee. I said to him that I need to get back to my university books and expand my knowledge of Eastern religions and Eastern philosophy. He offered to send me some titles that he has read. He was certainly challenging my boundaries.

## Buddhists 2 Catholics 0
## The CWA meeting

The regular group of ladies were in attendance. As expected the topic of Father Ryan came up and they all expressed their shock, horror and disappointment. Eventually, I asked them if they would feel better if they could ask questions anonymously. They agreed. They were each given a pen and sheets of paper to write their questions. Mabel would pick them up and read them out and I would answer to the best of my ability:

Q: "Will Father Ryan go to jail?"
A: "If there is enough evidence to convict him, then he will go to jail. Jails are a problem for sex offenders as they are mistreated and sexually abused."
Q: "Does he have a lawyer?"
A: "Yes, the Bishop has hired a good lawyer who happens to be Catholic. His name is Paul Taylor."
Q: "Is the Church reviewing the requirement of a male celibate priesthood?"
A: "No, in spite of it being a requested topic since 1960 of Bishops from around the world."
Q: "Has the sex abuse crisis in the Church opened the door to such a discussion?"
A: "Not yet."

Q. "Do you think the Church's attitude to women is discriminatory?"

A. "Yes. You will remember that I was married to Wendy, a strong feminist. She was very critical of the Catholic Church's attitude to women."

Q: "How can you stand working in a patriarchal church with such a negative view of women?"

A. "It is not easy but I am patiently waiting for women like you in the CWA to get out of your passive role in the Church, write our Bishop and the Pope complaining of their negative attitude towards women and demanding change. Nothing will change in the Catholic Church until you assume authority over this matter and demand a major structural change. The core teaching of the Church of love, forgiveness and tolerance is a very powerful message that I practice every day and that gives me great consolation."

Q: "If priests were allowed to marry, would we be having such a large problem with sexual abuse?"

A: "No. I do not think it would be as big a problem as we have had for the last 50 years."

Q: "In your opinion, why is the Catholic Church so resistant to change?"

A: "The problem is with the leadership of the Catholic Church. It lacks accountability and transparency. Archbishops and Cardinals live very privileged lives and are not accountable to anyone except the Pope. Having worked in government for many years, large organizations and institutions like the Catholic Church are very hard to govern. One answer might be to have an independent board of advisers comprised of ordinary lay Catholic men and women that the Pope, the Bishops and the Vatican are accountable to."

Q. "Are not the clergy supposed to be the servants of the Church?"

A. "Yes."

Q. "It is my opinion that a celibate clergy is generally out of touch with the lives of ordinary Catholics, would you not agree?"

A. "Priests learn about family life in the confessional. But I generally find it hard to answer that question."

Q: "Having been married, how has your marital relationship affected the way you operate as a priest?"

A: "While celibate priests are trained to live and work alone, my marriage to Wendy, although short-lived, taught me to share the decision-making of my work as a priest. I now believe that the parishioners and I are a team and I try to consult you often and share decision-making with you."

Q: "When will the Church allow women priests?"

A: "I do not know but I work with Claire an Anglican priest and Joan a United Church minister. We are good friends and members of an Interdenominational study group. They are very competent leaders. There exists an organization of women priests called Roman Catholic Women Priests (RCWP). They are validly ordained by some Bishops who took it upon themselves to ordain them. The Vatican has excommunicated them but they do not seem to care about the endorsement of the Vatican. There are approximately 145 of them in the world."

Q. "Why is God referred to as a male or a man? Is that Church teaching?"

A. "The Bible was written during a patriarchal era where men had more status in society at the time. So, from an historical perspective, God is described and written as a "He" or "Him". In the last century, women have gained equal status as men in society. Unfortunately, the Catholic Church is slow to change. But the answer to your question is that God is neither male or female. God is non-binary. Unfortunately, we do not have the words to describe God as both male and female."

After what seemed like forever, the questions ceased. I was able to bring up to date on other parish and community news: Mabel apologized for not having anything to say about the Developing Nations Aid Program. She has reached out to Claire and Joan. She informed the committee about the Anglicans renting space in St Francis. Liz asked for more time for anonymous questions:

Q: "Can non-Catholics receive the Eucharist at our Catholic masses?"

A: "Yes, they can as long as believe that Jesus is fully present body and soul in the Eucharist."

Q: "Can we receive the Eucharist if we attend their mass?"

A: "Yes, of course. Claire is a validly ordained priest according to Catholic teaching. She has the same priestly powers that I do. The key difference between the Catholic and the Anglican Church is that the Archbishop of Canterbury and the King and Queen of England are the heads of their Church, whereas the Pope is our head."

I also informed them that the Anglicans want to put a Christmas creche in our Church if we do not already have one. I then inquired if St. Francis had its own Christmas creche that was set up during this festive season? No one seemed to know. Mabel thought it was a good idea to let them provide that. She also wanted to know where the children's religious instruction program was at? I apologized and admitted that I had dropped the ball. I assured her that I would bring it up at the next Pastoral Council meeting.

I informed them that the Interdenominational study group wants to have a community Christmas dinner for the community at large. I advised them that I heartily supported the idea. It would take place on Tuesday, December 21 at the high school gym, 6:00 pm. There will books as gifts for the children. I hope that St. Francis will get behind this wonderful initiative. Claire and Joan are coordinating it.

### Women 2, Men 0

As we ended our meeting, Mabel reported that Susan is seven months pregnant and is doing well with Isabella. She will be finished her legal assistant training in early December. The baby is due is early January. Susan again expressed her appreciation for the love and support especially the financial support during her pregnancy from the CWA. Mabel asked the members present if she could write an article about Susan, protecting her identity, of course, for the CWA monthly National magazine called, Women of Faith? They voted yes unanimously.

Jerome emailed me requesting the 10:00 am Saturday time slot.

Father in heaven, thank you again for Don, Ed, the CWA ladies and Jerome coming into my life today. Please continue to guide me as I serve you and these wonderful parishioners. I pray for the Pope, the leadership of the Church, Bishop Ben, my parishioners, my family, the lonely, the depressed, the sick and the homeless. Keep them in your love.

### Thursday, November 25
### Pastoral Council meeting,

> Mantra for the Day:
>
> "If anyone says, 'I love God but hates his brother, he is a liar; for whoever does not love a brother whom he has seen, cannot love God whom he has not seen. Whoever loves God must also love his brother.'" (First letter of John, ch. 4, v. 20-21).

Bishop Ben emailed me today to share the contents of a telephone call he received from the Cardinal. The Bishop stated that during a discussion of Father Ryan, he was gently reprimanded by the Cardinal for not challenging the charges laid by the police. Children at the age of these victims have very active imaginations especially where there is stress and emotional pain involved. Our imagination is a faculty that can minimize emotional pain and even distort our recollection of the events. The Bishop implied that the Cardinal was critical of his handling of this situation and had let the Church down. Bishops are supposed to protect the Church from attacks from both within and without. He even hinted that had he been more aggressive, Father Ryan might still be an active priest today.

I reassured the Bishop that contrary to the Cardinal's point of view, I thought he had handled this situation ethically and professionally. As a former social worker, I expressed a view that by allowing the process to unfold as it did, he had avoided revictimizing these boys and their families at Court. Our lawyer, Paul Taylor was adamant that Father Ryan received a fair hearing. I also mentioned that Father Ryan's refusal to talk could be implied as guilt and remorse. He would always be a risk to the Diocese.

## Pastoral Council meeting

We had a full house. We spent a considerable amount of time dealing with everyone's shock and dismay regarding Father Ryan. They further questioned the wisdom of having him incarcerated in their town. I tried to re-assure them that as he was in police custody, he was no danger to anyone or anyone's children. The Bishop is worried that he may commit suicide. The men's club will be organizing a visiting program with him.

Next came the discussion on the Anglicans renting our Church. They also want to put up a creche of the Christmas stable scene over the holidays. After a short discussion, the Council agreed.

I also advised them that Rev. Joan White from the United Church had indicated at our last Interdenominational meeting that like the Anglicans, her declining number of parishioners was putting the survival of their parish church at risk. She too had inquired if their Church rent space from St. Francis. I had assured her that they would always be welcome at St. Francis but that I would need to confirm it with the Bishop and the members of the Pastoral Council.

Like the CWA, the discussion ranged from Anglicans being allowed to receive the Eucharist at our masses as long as they understood that the body and blood of Christ is present in the Eucharist. Little debate followed that discussion. Mabel informed everyone of a discussion item at their last CWA meeting. Why is God referred to as male or masculine? She concluded her comments by saying that we need to find a new way of referring to God that was neither male or female but both. Her comments were for information only and not for discussion purposes.

The big question was the new chicken processing plant coming to the community, the need for more housing and the land development opportunities for the residents of the town. I informed the group that the Town Administration has employed a retired city planner to coach them through their decision making.

I raised the matter of religious instruction for the children of the parish. I suggested that we begin by starting having a simple family style mass in their homes once a week. It would be based on the model of the last supper of Jesus with his apostles, which was the first Mass. We would begin with dinner, then Mass beginning with asking God to forgive our sins, then a Gospel reading from a children's bible that everyone could understand and would feel free to contribute, then shortened prayers of the Mass, the Our Father, communion, all in one hour. Fred wanted to know if this has been done before and I assured him that priest military chaplains use abbreviated forms of the Mass as soldiers can be called into battle on short notice. I will put a notice in the bulletin and please email me when I could come to your home for such a Mass.

The meeting ended with my announcing the community Christmas dinner and my hope that St. Francis would contribute in every way to make it happen. Claire and Joan were coordinating it.

I emailed Claire thanking her for offering to put up the creche and that we were in total support.

Father in heaven, thank you for another good day of activities for you. Keep the members of the Pastoral Council in your love. As always, I pray for Pope Francis, the bishops of the Church, my parishioners, my family, my friends, the sick, the tired, the public servants in our community, the lonely, the homeless and the dying. Thank you.

## Friday, November 26
## Samaritan Club meeting,

Mantra for the Day:

"Whatever you ask the Father in my name he will give to you. Until now you have not asked anything in my name; ask and you shall receive, so that your joy may be complete" (Gospel of John, ch.16, v. 23-24).

In preparation for the Samaritan Club meeting, I decided that the first item in our meeting was to eat our meal, then pray, like Christ and the Apostles did at the last supper. I emailed Jerome and Raymond and asked them to prepare the two readings, one from Luke on the lost sheep and the other from John on love. They agreed.

Mabel phoned me asking if we could meet this afternoon at Tim Horton's at 2:00 pm? Yes.

I arrived before she did. She walked in, stiff back, dressed to the "nines", every hair in place, a grey business suit, a red leather brief case and purse and finally red leather shoes. She began by explaining after some polite chitchat how much of a pleasure it has been to get to know both Claire and Joan. She has also become very distraught by the way the Catholic Church treats women. She reminded me that she has been a very loyal and committed Catholic for many years, especially as a member of the CWA. She admitted that she was not given to protests and placard-waving but instead has decided to challenge the Church through the Courts on their discriminatory attitude to women. She was not angry or critical at the Church leadership. She liked all the Bishops she had met, but thought that they were much too passive. Using the Courts may take longer but, in her opinion, is a more effective way to bring about change in the Church. When I asked her if she would have to resign from the CWA to take on this task, she replied that she would if she had to. Did I know a good lawyer for her? I gave her Paul Taylor's name and his toll-free telephone number and then suggested that she talk to Ed Malone, who is a good friend of the Cardinal in Toronto. The meeting was over and she was gone. My Tim's coffee still too hot to drink.

At 7:00 PM sharp, four cars entered our parking lot and six men and four women entered the rectory carrying containers of food. They went directly to the kitchen and took over the stove and oven. The aromas were rich and aromatic. Within ten minutes we were feasting on a main course of spicy Italian pasta with shrimp, stemmed broccoli and asparagus wrapped in bacon, served with a Pinot Grigio Italian white wine. A cheese tray followed, a small Caesar salad and a small piece of New York cheesecake for dessert. Totally delicious.

We cleared the dishes off the table and were again seated. I lit the candles and asked them to spend a few moments of silence to be mindful of our human failings as we prepared to celebrate the Eucharist. Jerome read the reading from the

Gospel of Luke on how Jesus cured a man with leprosy and Raymond read from one of the Letters of John where he says that where there is love, there is God. God is love. God enables us to love one another. A lively discussion followed on what these readings meant to them. There were even tears of joy. I reminded them that God loved them as they are and knew each by name. I assured them that they would always be welcome here at St. Francis as long as I was here. The Eucharistic prayer followed, then the Our Father, the Kiss of peace and the Eucharist. It was the shortest mass that I have ever celebrated. They looked a little surprised by the informality and the brevity. They cleaned up the kitchen and the dishes and were ready to leave by 9:00 pm when I asked for a few minutes of their time. I informed them about the community Christmas dinner and asked them if they would like to participate. They quickly agreed to assist.

Jerome also reminded me that he would be back tomorrow Saturday at 10:00 am. I reported to him that there would be twelve men attending the first cooking course.

Father in heaven, what a beautiful moving religious experience this evening. That must have been what the apostles experienced too with Jesus on Holy Thursday. These men and women are so kind and thoughtful. I wondered if the pain and struggle to "come out" has humanized them in a special way.

## Saturday/Sunday, November 27/28
## Preach on the Gospel of Luke

Mantra for Saturday and Sunday:

"Blessed are the poor, for the kingdom of God is yours. Blessed are you who are now hungry, for you will be satisfied" (Gospel of Luke, ch. 6, v. 20-21).

10:00 am, Jerome and Raymond were at my door with big smiles. They began by thanking me for the special mass last evening. All were moved by the warmth and the love they experienced. But they had barely seated themselves before I could even offer tea or coffee when they blurted out that they would like to be married in St. Francis. Would this be a problem? I could see my hands being tied behind my back, based on our discussion at the Thursday Samaritan Club meeting. I asked them how many people would be coming? That answer depended on my response to their request. I answered that I would love to bless their marriage but the Catholic Church does not as yet support gay marriages. The Bishop would do the responsible thing and sabotage the whole idea. Would you consider a small private Church wedding at St Francis and a large public reception in the City with family and friends? How many is small? Immediate members of your respective families or very close friends? I suggested a maximum of twenty people. They looked at each other and then back at me with a certain disbelief and disappointment in their eyes. I was obviously raining on their parade. Sensing some frustration, I asked them to leave it with me. I would contact the Bishop and get back to them. They agreed, turned down my offer of tea or coffee, thanked me again and said that the Samaritan Club would love to contribute to the Community Christmas dinner. They were off.

I emailed the Bishop's office, asking for some time with the Bishop. I phoned Father Mike and explained the request of Jerome and Raymond. I have requested a meeting with the Bishop on this matter and could he please come with me? He promised to make himself available.

## Saturday and Sunday Masses.
## Preaching on the Gospel of Luke

*"My dear friends, thank you for coming to Mass today. It is so nice to see you here on your day off from your work. My subject today is the Gospel of Luke. All the four gospel writers had a particular focus or theme in writing their accounts of Jesus. Luke was no exception. According to my research, there are four key elements to Luke's Gospel message. The first is that a spiritual life with God our father is available to all because He has created us all to share his life with us and wants a relationship with each and every one of us. The Old Testament is filled with stories about God the Father's relationships with us; to name just a few that I have discussed with you previously, would include Adam and Eve, Abraham, Noah, Joseph and Moses. The only problem is with our fear and apprehension to accept and respond to His invitations.*

*The second theme is the role of the Holy Spirit. The Holy Spirit is involved in the birth of Jesus, leads him into the desert and empowers his disciples to preach the Gospel. Like with Jesus, the Holy Spirit only speaks to us when we are silent and can listen.*

*The third theme is joy. Joy is the benefit of our relationship with Jesus. The birth of Jesus and of John the Baptist are portrayed as occasions of great joy. The return of outsiders or finding something that was lost are treated as joyful or special occasions.*

*The fourth theme is that God our Father is merciful and forgiving with our humanness and our failures to live up to our commitments to Him. Luke portrays Jesus' concern for those considered second class or outcasts namely women, the sick, the Samaritans (because they married non-Jewish persons).*

*Reading and reflecting on this Gospel can be very comforting to our daily struggles and our challenges."*

## Dinner with family:

These dinners can be unpredictable and this Sunday evening was no exception. To the benign question of my brother, "What is new in your world, Bro?", I told them about the request of these two gay men wanting to get married at St. Francis Church. Silence followed. The following conversation unfolded between my brother Jim and I:

- Q. "Cam have you ever had such a request before?"
- A. "No, never in my short experience as a priest."
- Q. "Does the Church bless gay marriages?"
- A. "No, it does not, mainly because the Church sees intimate relationships of gay men and women as sinful and wrong. The Church only blesses marriages of men with women. Some may call this being prejudiced against them. I agree."
- Q. "So, you said no, right?"
- A. "No, I did not."
- Q. "Why not?"
- A. "I thought that I should consult the Bishop first. They are fine men. Their relationship has lasted over ten years. They love one another and they are good upstanding citizens. I personally think the Church is out of step in these situations. It is judgemental and discriminatory in

not blessing their marriage. If Christ were alive today, I firmly believe that He would bless their marriage."
- Q. "So, you will be advocating having the Church bless their marriage, correct?"
- A. "Yes, I am."
- Q. "What reasons will you give the Bishop in support of having the Church bless their marriage?"
- A. "In addition to what I have already explained to you, God is love according to the Gospel of John. Since God is love and all love is from God. Their love is from God too. According to the Gospel of Luke, Christ focussed his time on earth with the disadvantaged, the poor, the outcastes. Our society has treated gays and lesbians as outcastes. The Gospel of Luke tells us not to judge one another. Pope Francis, our current Pope, is quoted as saying on this subject, "Who am I to judge?" Based on the above reasons, I will recommend that we bless their marriage."
- Q. "What if he says no?"
- A. "Father Mike and I are seeing the Bishop tomorrow late in the afternoon and we are even invited for dinner too. He cooks Italian. I am keeping an open mind on this matter."

Sis jumped in calling me a rebel. You will be destined forever to a little remote parish; out of sight, out of mind to the Bishop.

Dad: "Son, in my opinion, you are doing the right thing. Your honesty and forthrightness will assist you in the challenging days ahead. We are totally behind you. We are very proud of you."

Sis: "Come on Dad, you're giving him a swelled head and feeding his growing ego problem."

Mother: "We will pray for you, son," Her standard response.

Father in heaven, thank you for the love and honesty of my parents, my brother, my sister and my nieces and nephews. Thank you for another great day of service to our parishioners and your love of me.

## Monday, November 29
## Day off

Mantra for the Day:

"Blessed are the merciful, for they shall will be shown mercy" (Gospel of Matthew, ch. 5, v. 7).

Margaret emailed me and Father Mike stating that the Bishop gave us the last appointment of the day at 5:00 pm and reminded us that he wants us to stay for dinner too. He wants us to go straight to his apartment. He is cooking something special.

5:00 pm, the Bishop and Max welcomed me into his small apartment to the strong smell of garlic. The apartment was one large room with a separate bedroom and bathroom. He was wearing an Edmonton CFL football shirt under a very colourful but stained apron. As he hung up my coat, he said that he wanted us to eat and then talk. Father Mike arrived shortly after.

He explained that he was cooking Italian fish stew, including shrimp, calamari and oysters in a tomato sauce with fresh ciabatta bread. Yes, a Caesar salad too (beware: he overdoes the garlic), a penne pasta with a Bolognese sauce, chianti red wine and strong back Illy coffee so that we would arrive home safely. He also warned us that we might not be able to sleep right away!

The dinner was exactly as Margaret had predicted. It was delicious but loaded with garlic that cleared out my sinuses. We moved to his living room for more wine and coffee. We had barely sat down when he announced that he has been promoted. He was asked and has agreed to become the new Archbishop of Quebec. He starts January 01. He continued that he has accepted this promotion on the condition that either of you become his successor. The Vatican has reluctantly agreed to consider this request as they normally do not operate that way. His main argument was that either of you know the complex and challenging situations this diocese is dealing with. Once he had outlined to the Vatican representatives concerning the many problems and issues, they reluctantly agreed to consider it. Regarding my replacement, they will be contacting you shortly for your input on this important decision. My issue; my blessing of a gay marriage paled by comparison.

Bishop Ben turned to me and asked what it was that I wanted to discuss with him. I outlined the request of Jerome and Raymond, their character and their fine qualities, the length of their relationship, their contribution to the LGBTQIA+ community and to the parish. I concluded that it would be a private ceremony with only close family and friends. I recommended that we bless their marriage and give them the love and support we normally give every normal Catholic relationship.

The Bishop then turned to Father Mike. After what seemed like an unusually long pause, he asked if we could keep it out of the press and from Ed Malone, the Cardinal's friend. I assured them that I could manage those requirements. Father Mike looking at the Bishop, stated that this could fall under the "ad experimentum", a Latin term for the Vatican's new approach to trying out innovative Church practices based on long overdue requests from Bishops. He also wanted to know if we refused to bless their marriage, would they go to the press and give us a black eye. I stated that was clearly a possibility, but only remote. I thought that our decision should be based on good biblical theology and because both are baptized Catholics in good standing, we should support them.

Father Mike asked if they had completed a pre-marriage instruction course. I did not know.

After more discussion, the Bishop decided that given their age, the length of their relationship and their agreement to take a pre-marriage course within six months, their marriage could be blessed in a small private ceremony at St. Francis Church.

I closed the discussion by stating that they were planning a private reception in the city for family and friends.

Father in heaven, thank you for another day in your service. Thank you for Bishop Ben (and Max, of course), Father Mike, Margaret, Jerome, Raymond, good garlic laced Italian food, Italian wine and strong black coffee. Time to watch the highlights of the Monday night NFL game.

## Tuesday, November 30
## Scripture Study, The Gospel of Mark,

> Mantra for the day:
>
> "Listen carefully to what I am saying and be wary of the shrewd advice that tells you how to get ahead in the world on your own. Giving, not getting, is the way. Generosity begets generosity. Stinginess narrows one"
> (Gospel of Mark, ch. 4, v. 24-25).

### Gospel of Mark Summary notes:

1. The Gospel of Mark is another portrait of Jesus.
2. Mark is believed to have been an associate of Peter, the Apostle.
3. This Gospel was written around the time of the destruction of Jerusalem in 70 CE.

4. It was the first Gospel to be written and was a source for the Gospels of Matthew and Luke.
5. According to some authorities, the Gospels were written to meet the needs of the early Christians. Mark's dual picture of Jesus as compared to the other three Gospel writers reveals a Jesus on the one hand who is performing many wonderful miracles and on the other hand reveals a human side of Jesus who experiences many human emotions.
6. The key message is simple but demanding. It centres on Christ's suffering and death and the meaning of suffering. To be a follower of Christ requires a radical trust in God and the loving service of the needs of others.
7. Mark's Gospel best reveals the human side of Jesus and his many emotional states. For example, Jesus was deeply grieved and angry and was indignant. He loves the rich man. He is discouraged by his follower's inability to understand him and his mission. Jesus is troubled and distressed in the Garden of Gethsemane just prior to his suffering and death.
8. Anyone searching for the meaning of life from a Christian perspective can turn to where is summed up: The meaning of life and happiness is in accepting suffering in the imitation of the suffering Jesus in spite of the challenges and difficulties they entail. Serve the needs of your fellow men even in the face of death.

I emailed Father Mike requesting a meeting on Wednesday. He replied that he was available at 10.00 am at his rectory.

As Ned left, he asked if I was free for lunch tomorrow. Could he pick up a pizza from Mario's? Yes, of course.

I emailed Jerome to say that the Bishop has given the go-ahead for their wedding in St. Francis provided it was a small family affair and there were no representatives of the press in attendance. He suggested that if you guys, your family and friends want to party afterwards, please, as we had agreed, do it in the City. The Bishop also wanted the assurance that you and Raymond would take a pre-marriage course with six months of the wedding. What date and time would you like your wedding to take place? Would you want a simple wedding ceremony or in conjunction with a celebration of the Eucharist?

Father in heaven, thank you for the strong message in the Gospel of Mark. Thank you for all you do for me. Thank you for family, friends and parishioners. Please keep the Pope, the Bishops and my fellow priests close to your heart. Special thoughts and prayers for Bishop Ben in his new appointment. Help all those stressed out, the worried, the sick and the lonely to find peace and rest.

# CHAPTER 2

# *Journal Entries for December*

---

## Wednesday, December 01
## Office work

Mantra for the day:

"The Lord is faithful in all his words, and gracious in all his deeds. The Lord upholds all who are falling, and raises up all who are bowed down. The eyes of all look to you, and you give them their food in due season." (Book of Psalms, ch. 145, v. 13b–15)

I met Father Mike at 10:00 am. We had a productive discussion on the state of the diocese as he has been acting second in command for more than ten years. We agreed that until the Vatican appoints someone to replace Bishop Ben, that I would take the lead in the administration of the diocese and he would be my back-up. He reminded me again that he has been diagnosed with coronary artery disease. This is a condition in which heart muscles do not get enough blood and oxygen. He could die at any time without warning. Losing him during this time of transition would be damaging for the diocese. He will be my back up as long as his health will permit. I thanked him again for his kindness to me and his service to the diocese. He continued that the diocese would be in good hands if you continue to operate like you do in St. Francis by listening and consulting frequently and delegating more.

We then talked about organizing a farewell for Bishop Ben. Given the Bishop's preference for a quiet, informal gathering, we agreed on Wednesday, December 29 for two events: one a stand-up lunch 11:30 am to 1:30 pm in the Cathedral boardroom for the priests of the diocese and a second one, a "Come and Go" event from 7:00 pm to 9:00 pm in the Cathedral boardroom for the laity (non-clerical persons of the diocese) and public officials. We will ask Margaret to organize both with appropriate newspaper notices. No gifts either.

Ned was waiting for me when I returned from the city. He is such a nice person and I sense he is very accommodating of Mabel and the families of their two daughters. He asked me what I had said to Mabel the other day. Why? She has spent literally the last four days with Claire and Joan. I reminded him that they are working on the Developing Nations Program. Ned thought there was something more going on. Mabel has told him that she might need to use some family money for a cross Canada CWA visitation. She also mentioned a challenge through the Courts of the Church's ill-treatment of women. She mentioned that Paul Taylor has agreed to represent their group. Ned has heard that Taylor is a formidable lawyer. She is organizing a petition of both men and women in support of this Court challenge. When I asked her what she would do if men refused to sign. She was adamant, "If you love me, you will sign. If you don't, you will get no love and affection from me,"

Wow. I was blown away. Better not get into her bad books. She is formidable too.

Ned continued that she had mentioned Ed Malone too.

I suspect he responded like a lapdog. More award-winning feature articles for the Toronto Tribune. We sat in silence letting all this sink in.

Finally, Ned began that after reflecting on their conversation over the weekend, he will support anything and everything that Mabel does. He has spent considerable time away from Mabel and the girls working on the international stage in his career with her support. She raised their two girls alone. Now it was her turn to shine and he would support her all the way. I assured him that it was the absolute right thing to do under the circumstances.

He then asked me how I felt about this potential Court challenge. I replied that whatever helped to present Christ's message better, I would support. I would support Mabel wholeheartedly.

3:00 pm, I attended another meeting at the Town office for a working session of the Town's expansion plans. Present were Todd Joseph, the Town Manager, Stanley Robinson, Consultant, William Blake, the Town Engineer and Mary Jones, secretary and me. We agreed on the following: the location of the new chicken processing plant should be located downwind from the town, a variety of housing types were needed including coop housing where the Town owned the land and the residents only owned the building, small apartments, townhouses and regular single detached housing with ample parks and open space. We agreed to meet again in a week.

Fred Bartlett emailed me requesting some time tomorrow, if possible. We agreed to meet at 1:00 am the next day.

7:30 pm: the first of the three cooking lessons for the men of the parish began in the hospital kitchen. Jerome, Raymond and Timothy were leading. Present were Ned, Fred, Bill, Jim, Tom, Colin, Ed Malone and me. There were three no-shows. Their instruction included the basic such as steaming, blanching, poaching and braising, very healthy cooking techniques without requiring expertise or an array of gadgets. They demonstrated these techniques with a variety of meats, vegetables and fruits. They also covered grilling, broiling, baking, roasting and sautéing. Their handouts were excellent. They finished at 10:00 pm.

Father in heaven, what should I be doing to help Father Mike? Suggesting that he give up parish work and retire before he is ready could have very negative consequences. Please continue to guide me in my work with him, Jerome and Raymond, Ned and Mabel, the Town planning committee and with Fred and Thelma.

## Thursday, December 02
## More office work

> "Behold, I stand at the door and knock, says the Lord. If anyone hears my voice and opens the door to me, I will enter his house and dine with him, and he with me" (Book of Revelations, ch. 3, v. 20).

At 10:00 am Fred and Thelma arrived looking very distraught. They waved off coffee or tea and got to the point of their visit. Hilary's mother, Rose, 96 years of age has taken a turn for the worse. She suffers from macular degeneration and is virtually blind and quite deaf. She lives in a long-term care home in the city that seems to be understaffed. They have found her occasionally sitting in soiled clothes. She has expressed for some time a strong desire to end her life. We have tried to quietly discourage this but she has stopped eating four days ago. As she is not in pain, the use of morphine, that can speed up one's death, is not recommended. Her doctor is very sympathetic and believes that he has done all he can do for her. She now meets all the medical prerequisites for a doctor-assisted death.

Fred asked if she could receive a Christian burial if they were to support her desire to die now. I assured them both that this was a very difficult situation but whatever decision the three of you make, I will support you wholeheartedly and will ensure you that she has a Christian burial here at St. Francis.

At 1:00 pm, Claire arrived as scheduled with Stella, her parish assistant. We toured the Church, the sacristy and the meeting room in my mobile home. I showed them the closets and drawers in the sacristy where the vestments were located, the chalices, the ciboria, the patens, altar linens etc. They had a lot of questions which seemed to reflect more their anxiety than a need to know. We had tea and I gave them a set of keys for church and rectory doors as well as the locked cabinets where we stored the sacred vessels. They seemed pleased. As they were leaving, I said that I would not be surprised that Catholics may turn up at her services. I asked her if they celebrated the Eucharist to which she replied yes. As they parted, she said that she would welcome them "with open arms".

At 3:00 pm, the Interdenominational Group met in the rectory. It was a special meeting to discuss the plans for the community Christmas dinner. Claire and Joan reported that the gym had been booked and the Town Office would finance the dinner and gifts provided it would canvass funds from other groups in the community. The menu will consist of turkey, mashed potatoes, mixed vegetables, a salad and apple pie. The plan is for the Town to purchase the turkeys and the vegetables at cost once we know how many respondents we have. The turkeys and vegetables will be cooked in various kitchens. The Town library will supply the books as gifts. We have estimated a $5,000.00 to cover all the costs. Joan then asked if St. Francis could put up $1,000.00? I assured her that yes, we could do that. I volunteered to roast a turkey too.

Father in heaven, thank you for another day in your service. Thank you for bringing Fred, Hilary, Rose, Claire, Stella and my Interdenominational group into my life. These people enrich my life. As usual, I pray for the Pope, the Bishops, my fellow priests, my family, my friends, the lonely, the depressed and the homeless. Keep them all in your loving embrace.

## Friday, December 03
## A quiet catch-up day

Mantra for the Day:

"God has created us to do some definite service. He has committed some work to me which he has not committed to another. I may never know it in this lifetime but I shall be told it in the next." St. John Henry Newman (1801 – 1890)

I visited Father Ryan again today but as before, he would not talk to me. It was disappointing because I am not his enemy. He apparently talks to no one. He does, however, play cribbage with Constable Melanie Campbell. I wonder if he should be seen by a psychiatrist or someone like Paul Taylor? I emailed the Bishop with these suggestions.

Father in heaven, thank you for a quiet day, allowing me to catch-up day with my laundry, reading for my scripture course and tidying my office and rectory. Guide me in my desire to assist Father Ryan in some helpful way. I cannot imagine what he is going through. Thank you for suggesting a psychiatrist.

## Saturday/Sunday, December 04/05

Mantra for the Day:

"The Lord is my shepherd, I shall not want. He makes me lie down in green pastures; he leads beside still waters; he restores my soul" (Book of Psalms, ch. 23, v. 1-3).

The Saturday edition of the Prairie News reported that St. Francis Parish was taking over the responsibility of snow shovelling the main sidewalks in the winter and the maintenance of two rinks, one for hockey and another for pleasure skating. The Editor, Ed Malone publicly thanked the St Francis Parish for taking on this responsibility. His newspaper also announced the community Christmas dinner scheduled for December 21. All are welcome. Please register with the newspaper, Prairie News by December 15.

I preached on the life of John the Baptist.

> "My dear friends, I thank you as I do regularly for coming to Mass today on your day off. You will be well rewarded for these efforts. My subject today is the unusual life of John, the Baptist. The story begins with his parents. His father Zechariah was a priest from the tribe of Levi, one of the original twelve tribes in Israel. He was a priest serving the Lord during the reign of Herod in Judea. He and his wife Elizabeth were described as blameless and kind. As the story begins, they are advanced in age and had no children as Elizabeth was barren (in this society, the wife was blamed). Zechariah, in accordance with his priestly duties, was chosen to enter the Holy Place of the Temple and burn incense to the Lord. During this event, the Angel Gabriel appeared to him and told him that he and Elizabeth had been chosen by God to have a son who would be the herald to usher in the long-awaited Messiah. They were to consecrate him as a servant of God and were to name him John. In spite of the good news, Zechariah was skeptical and did not believe Gabriel. He responded that such was impossible because he and his wife

*were too old and beyond childbearing. Can you blame him?. Due to his disbelief, Gabriel told him that he would become mute until the prophesy could be fulfilled when the baby was circumcised. Zechariah was immediately unable to speak and when he came out of the Temple, he had to communicate with hand gestures. Those outside the Temple realized that he had seen a vision.*

*Zechariah returned home and soon according to God's plan, Elizabeth became pregnant. She entered into seclusion for five months. Soon, Mary conceived Jesus and upon hearing that Elizabeth was pregnant, went with haste to visit her.*

*After John was born and it was time for his circumcision, the family thought he should be named after Zechariah, the father. Elizabeth objected and wanted the name John. When the family turned to Zechariah, he using a writing tablet, wrote that his name is John. Immediately he was able to speak and praise God.*

*There are other stories of significant events in the Old testament where women are barren but God uses their barren-ness to fulfill his plan for humanity. Sara, Abraham's barren wife, became the mother of the Islamic, Jewish and Christian dynasties with the birth of Isaac. She too was at an age well beyond child bearing when she became pregnant. Others include Rebecca (Isaac's wife), Rachel (Jacob's wife), Hannah (mother of Samuel) and the anonymous wife of Manoah (mother of Samson). God our father seems to be using these unusually late pregnancies to highlight his interventions into our lives. Christianity had some very special features identifying it.*

*John's life was unusual too. He lived a life of prayer and solitude in the desert eating locusts and honey. The Canadian Food Guide would not have been available to him at the time. The desert held a special meaning to the Jewish people from their days in the desert after being rescued from an oppressive Pharaoh. His role was to announce the beginning of Jesus' public life until he was beheaded by Herod. John was eventually beheaded by Herod because John criticized him for living with his brother's wife.*

*A takeaway from this Mass, is that we need to build prayer time or meditation into our lives enabling God, our loving Father in heaven to enter into our lives. He wants to make our lives better and to use us to benefit others. If we give Him a chance to enter our lives and live by His guidelines, our lives will be special and the lives of those around us will become special as well."*

## Dinner with family

While the four grandchildren were excited about another Christmas and a trip to San Diego, I was able to alert the adults of Bishop Ben' immanent departure on January 01. To their question of who would be replacing him, I replied that the Vatican was very slow in replacing Bishops. In the meantime, Father Mike, in poor health and I would jointly fill in until that replacement is determined. Would I still be coming to San Diego with them? Yes, I would but perhaps not for the amount of time that I had originally planned. Mother had prepared a delicious pot roast, mashed potatoes, parsnips, green peas and strawberry-rhubarb pie for dessert. Dad had recovered from that nasty cold and flu. They quietly confessed that they were able to arrange three days at Disneyland in Anaheim, California. I informed them of the community Christmas dinner scheduled for December 21 at 6:00 pm in the school gym and invited them all to come and experience a warm community meal. I explained all the details and asked mother's help in cooking a sixteen-pound turkey. They agreed to consider it. I dropped off $300.00 with my brother and sister for gifts for the four nieces and nephews. I suggested that we draw names of the adult gifts.

Father in heaven, thank you for the following opportunities today; the gift to be able to talk about John the Baptist and his parents, for the brief visits with the parishioners after the masses and finally time to be with my family. Thank you for the continuing health of my aging parents.

## Monday December 06
## My Day off

Mantra for the day:

"To live is to change and to be perfect, is to have changed often." St. John Henry Newman (1801 – 1890)

At 10:00 am, Father Raj arrived for his pre-scheduled appointment. He has been under medical supervision by both his family doctor and a psychiatrist for over two weeks. They are recommending an immediate leave of absence for a minimum of two months. They have assessed him as exhausted, being emotionally burned-out and severely stressed. His health is at risk. Should he inform the Bishop? I explained that Bishop Ben has been appointed as the new Archbishop of Quebec and would be leaving on January 01. Father Mike and I will be managing the diocese until a new Bishop is assigned. I suggest that you alert him to your situation and let him know that you and I have been talking. It will be an opportunity for you to say good bye to him privately. I also advised Raj to chat with Claire, our Anglican minister in town. They have sold their church and will be renting space in St. Francis. Considering that his church and rectory have burned down, he might want to recommend to his parishioners to consider renting space from another religious group in the community.

Margaret sent an email inviting all diocesan priests to a special meeting with Bishop Ben Wednesday morning, December 08, in the Cathedral boardroom at 10:00 am.

Father in heaven, thank you for another day in your service. Thank you for all the good people who are in my life, especially Fathers Raj and Mike, Claire, Margaret, Fred, Thelma, Susan, Maggie, my family and my parishioners. Keep them all in your love and protection.

# December 07
# Scripture Study "Joseph, the earthly father of Jesus",

Mantra for the Day:

"An angel of the Lord appeared to him in a dream and said, "Joseph, son of David, do not be afraid to take Mary as your wife, for the child conceived in her is from the Holy Spirit. She will bear a son and you are to name him Jesus, for he will save his people from their sins. When Joseph awoke from sleep, he did as the angel of the Lord had commanded; he took Mary as his wife" (Gospel of Matthew, ch.1, v. 20-24).

# Scripture study: Joseph, the Earthly Father of Jesus

## Summary of notes:

- Joseph was the earthly father of Jesus and the husband of Mary, Jesus' mother. As lineage is very important for Israelites, Joseph's lineage is traced back to King David. It is thought that he was born around 100 B.C.E. and died around 1 C.E.
- In the stories of Jesus and Mary, Joseph plays the role of protector, husband and father and provider.
- After they became engaged, Joseph found out Mary was already pregnant. Unwilling to bring shame on her as he was a kind and just man Joseph decided to divorce her quietly. He feared that if he were to do it publicly, she would be stoned to death.
- Still only engaged and at some risk, the pregnant Mary nevertheless, departed to the hill country to visit her cousin Elizabeth who had become pregnant late in life with John the Baptist.
- Finally, an angel of God came to Joseph in a dream (the first of four visits) telling him that the child Mary carried was the son of God and was conceived by the Holy Spirit. Joseph completed the marriage ceremony and took Mary for his wife.
- Then, Emperor Augustus orders a census. Joseph and Mary, being law-biding citizens make this awkward journey to Bethlehem, Joseph's ancestral city.
- Bethlehem was overcrowded with many committed to completing the census. Mary and Joseph ultimately found accommodation in a stable with animals. There Jesus was born.
- After Jesus' birth, an angel of God came to Joseph in a dream (the second time) warning him of King Herod's desire to kill the infant Jesus and all infant male children.

The angel requested that he take Jesus and his mother Mary and flee quickly to Egypt. They were to remain there until it was safe to return. That would have been a very arduous trip for Mary especially having just given birth to a child.
- After Herod's death, an angel of God came to Joseph in a dream (the third such visit) telling him it was safe to return to Israel but another angel tells him to reside in Galilee in the town of Nazareth. There it was thought that he worked as a carpenter.
- Joseph and Mary fulfill their religious duties regarding circumcision and the presentation of their first born to the Lord. At the Temple, they encounter Simeon and Anna, two old faithful Israelites who recognize Jesus as the Messiah. Jesus is described as the "light of the nations".
- Then, Joseph's role in the family ends. He is mentioned vaguely when he and Mary took Jesus to Jerusalem for the annual Passover festival when Jesus was twelve years old. It is assumed that he had died before the Jesus' crucifixion as Jesus from the cross asked John to care for his mother.

Father in heaven, thank you for another special day. Thank you.

# Wednesday, December 08
# Bishop Ben meets priests of the Diocese

> "Whenever you pray, go into your room and shut the door and pray to your Father who is in secret and your father who sees in secret will reward you" (Gospel of Matthew, ch. 6, v. 6).

The 10:00 am time meeting with the Bishop began on time in spite of the laughter and chatter of priests catching up with one another. He announced that sadly, he would be leaving the diocese as he has been appointed Archbishop of Quebec effective immediately. He confessed that he was finally managing this diocese in a respectable manner and was hoping to spend many years growing old here. Margaret however, would be staying through this transition. Max will stay with her and become her companion. He turned and thanked Margaret for her many dedicated years of service to the diocese. He then called her up to the front and gave her a beautiful bouquet of red roses, one for each year of service and a kiss on both cheeks. He continued that until a new Bishop is announced, Father Mike and Father Cam will jointly administer the diocese. Father Mike has the experience and Father Cam has the energy. They will be a fabulous tag team. I asked for the floor and then explained that Father Mike and I were organizing two modest farewells for the Bishop. One, a light lunch for the clergy on December 29, 11:30 am to 1:30 pm in the Cathedral boardroom and a second for the laity in the evening, a "come and go" 7:00 pm to 9:00 pm in the Cathedral boardroom. The Bishop thanked us and said that Margaret will be contacting the local newspapers to formally announce these changes.

At 3:00 pm a small group hesitatedly entered my boardroom with large maps and drawings. They were Todd Joseph, the Town Manager, William (Bill) Blake, the Town Engineer, Stanley Robinson, formerly retired but now employed Town Planner,

Mary Jones, the secretary and Ed Malone. The meeting focussed on finalizing a new town plan with a zoning bylaw that would guide the new developments that would occur once the plan was approved by the Province and by the Town Council.

They advised that they hoped to present this plan to Town Council in January and hoped that I would speak in support of the plan. I agreed. Ed would keep me informed as this plan was prepared for Town Council.

Tonight, was the second of three cooking lessons provided by the Samaritan Club for the men in St. Francis. The theme was Italian cooking and they outlined the essential ingredients: extra virgin olive oil, balsamic vinegar, garlic, pasta, pasta sauce, fresh tomatoes, oregano, parmesan cheese and capers. They also demonstrated the importance of chopping, dicing and slicing so that food was cooked at the same time. They capped the evening by making a special, to die for, pizza. That was in addition to the samples they brought of a few dishes for us to taste and served them with a Sangiovese red wine. A big success.

Father in heaven, thank you for today. I pray for Bishop Ben, all my fellow priests, Margaret, Max, the town planning folks and all your people who are sick, tired, overwhelmed, and afraid. Thank you for the Samaritan Club for putting on this cooking course for men in the parish. Does my love of Italian foods mean that I have lived a previous life in Italy? Continue to love and protect these wonderful gay men, please.

## Thursday, December 09
## Provincial Court

Mantra for the Day:

"I am the way, the truth and the life, says the Lord; no one comes to the Father, except through me. If you know me, you know the Father also" (Gospel of John, ch. 14, v. 6).

I joined the Bishop in Court to hear the Judge's decision concerning Father Ryan. He was found guilty on all accounts and sentenced to twenty-five years in a secured non-penitentiary institution where he will never be a danger to society. He could become eligible for parole in twenty-five years. The Court costs include five days of hearings ($20,000.00), pain and suffering compensation to each family ($200,000.00 totalling $400,000.00), individual and family counselling for each family ($200,000.00 totalling $400,000.00), an education fund for each family ($100,000.00 totalling $200,000.00) and legal fees honorarium of $5,000.00. The total cost is $1,0250,000.00. The Judge took Father Ryan's age and years of service as a priest in making his decision. Given that sexual offenders are vulnerable in our penitentiaries, he welcomed the Bishop's intervention in finding a suitable secure alternative with the Benedictines. When not in a secured facility, Father Ryan will be required by the Court to wear an electronic ankle bracelet.

I received an email from Maggie. She is returning home for Christmas on December 17. She will finally tell them about her pregnancy. She has decided against having an abortion. Could I be available to attend one or more family meetings as they come to terms with this matter? I assured her that I would except when called to carry out church responsibilities.

Father in heaven, thank you for Bishop Ben, Father Ryan, the Judge's decision, Maggie. Help us to see something beneficial from the Judge's decision regarding Father Ryan.

## Friday, December 10
## Office work and news about Father Raj.

Mantra for the Day:

"God loves each of us as if there were only one of us." St. Augustine (354-430 C E)

I emailed all members of the CWA, the Pastoral Council and the Men's group inviting them to a short meeting scheduled for Wednesday, December 15 at 7:00 pm in the Rectory boardroom.

I received an email from Claire today advising me that she and Father Raj had met yesterday. He explained his situation. She advised him that the Anglican Church does not poach priests from other dioceses but if he decided to get married and became unacceptable in the Catholic Church, they would welcome him into their diocese. This is very interesting.

## Saturday/Sunday, December 11/12
## Preach Joseph, the earthly father of Jesus

Mantra for the Day:

"The Lord is my rock, my fortress and my deliverer. My God, my rock in whom I take refuge, my shield, and the source of my salvation, my stronghold" (Book of Psalms, 18 : 2).

I preached about Joseph, the earthly father of Jesus:

*"My good friends, thank you for coming to Mass today. My subject today is Joseph, the earthly father of Jesus and the husband of Mary, Jesus' mother. As lineage in Jewish life was very*

*important, Joseph's lineage can be traced back to King David. It is thought that he was born around 100 B.C.E., married Mary, cared for Mary and Jesus and died about 1 C.E.*

*While the story of Joseph is vitally connected to Jesus and Mary, I wanted to focus on Joseph today. While engaged to Mary, he found out she was already pregnant. Being a kind and just man and unwilling to bring shame on her, he decided to divorce her quietly. He feared that if he were to do it publicly, she would be stoned to death as was the custom in his day.*

*But before Joseph could carry out his plan, an angel of God came to him in a dream (the first of four of them) telling him that the child Mary carried was the son of God and was conceived by the Holy Spirit. He was encouraged to take Mary as his wife in spite of these unusual circumstances. Joseph then took Mary for his wife completing the marriage ceremony.*

*After Jesus' birth in Bethlehem, an angel of God came to Joseph in a dream (the second time) warning him of King Herod's desire to kill all infant male children. The angel requested that he take Jesus and Mary and flee quickly to safety in Egypt. They were to remain there until he was advised it was safe to return.*

*After Herod's death, an angel of God came to Joseph in a dream (the third such visit) telling him it was safe to return to Israel but another angel tells him to reside in Galilee in the town of Nazareth. There it was thought that he worked as a carpenter.*

*When Jesus was a few weeks old, Joseph and Mary took him to the Temple in Jerusalem where he as a first-born male child, was presented God in accordance with Jewish Law. Similarly, this visit completed the purification of the mother again in compliance with Jewish Law. It was there that they met Simeon and Anna, two aged Jewish people who were waiting and praying for the long-anticipated arrival of the Messiah.*

*When Jesus is twelve years old, on an annual pilgrimage to the Temple, he became separated from Mary and Joseph. Thinking that Jesus was with their friends in the caravan, they travelled three days before they realized that in fact that he was not with them. Mary and Joseph finally found him the Temple conversing with a group of teachers. When Mary confronted Jesus how worried she and Joseph were, He dismissed their concerns indicating that He was dealing with matters important to His heavenly Father.*

*Joseph's role in the family ends. It is implied that he had died before the Crucifixion as Jesus from the cross asked John, the apostle to care for his mother.*

*Joseph is a good role model for us men. While there was nothing special about him, except that he was a provider and protector of Mary and Jesus. He was called to a special role of being the earthly father of Jesus and the husband of Mary. Many of us live out quiet ordinary lives like Joseph. We are called to provide calm leadership, generous love and strong protection for those in our lives who we love enabling them to grow and mature."*

### Sunday Dinner with Family

Sunday dinner was relaxing for a change. We were eleven; my parents, my sister, her husband and their two children and my brother, his wife and their two children. The house was filled with smells of mother's cooking and the noisy excitement of Christmas anticipated by the children. I reminded them of the Christmas dinner planned for the community, that they were invited too and that I needed to cook a sixteen-pound turkey for the occasion. I avoided any discussion on my world and kept it on the children's hopes for Christmas gifts. Before returning to the parish, Mother gave me detailed written instructions on how to roast a sixteen-pound turkey while I inhaled a piece of her apple pie and ice cream.

Father in heaven, thank you for your help with Joseph's story and a special thank you for my family but especially my mother and all mothers.

### Monday, December 13
### Day off

Mantra for the Day:

"O give thanks to the Lord, for he is good; for his steadfast love endures forever" (Book of Psalms, ch. 106, v. 1).

I emailed Margaret thanking her for agreeing to stay during this transition. Was there anything that we should know about or do prior to Bishop Ben's departure on January 01? Please advise. Thank you.

I received an email from Father Raj stating that he was spending a week with the Benedictines. After Father Joe welcomed him into the community, he was assigned kitchen duties. No slackers or free lunches with Father Joe.

## Tuesday, December 14
## Scripture study "Mary the mother of Jesus"

Mantra for the Day:

"Greetings, favored one! The Lord is with you. Do not be afraid, Mary, for you have found favor with God. And now you will conceive in your womb and bear a son and you will name him Jesus" (Gospel of Luke, ch. 1, v. 28-32).

### Summary notes: Mary (18 BCE – 41 CE)

What we know of Mary is from the four Gospels:

- Mary was betrothed to Joseph. They had formally agreed to marry and were considered husband and wife but were not living together;
- The Angel Gabriel visited Mary requesting her consent to become the mother of Jesus, the Son of God, the long-awaited Messiah of the Jewish people. She will become pregnant through the power of the Holy Spirit. She accepts the invitation. She learns at the same time that her cousin Elizabeth previously barren, is now pregnant in her old age.
- Given her role as the mother of Jesus, Catholics believe that Mary was born without original sin. This condition is called an Immaculate Conception. She is also known as the blessed Virgin Mary. While she married, she is believed to have remained a virgin throughout her life. There is no actual evidence of this.

- Joseph, on discovering Mary's pregnancy, was prepared to divorce her quietly but that when told in a dream that she conceived by the power of the Holy Spirit, he should not hesitate to take her as his wife. He did, completing the wedding ritual;
- Mary rushed to visit Elizabeth in Hebron, the hill country of Judah to help her for three months;
- The Roman Emperor Augustus required that Joseph return to his hometown of Bethlehem to register for a Roman census. While there, Jesus was born in a stable as there was no room in the local Marriott hotels (approximately 6 BCE). Mary used a manger for a crib. Jesus is welcomed into the world by poor itinerant shepherds;
- Sometime after his birth, three Magi, astrologers probably from Babylon, came to worship Jesus and acknowledge Him as their savior;
- After eight days, Jesus was circumcised according to the Jewish law and given the name of Jesus, meaning Yahweh is salvation;
- After the departure of the Magi, Joseph was warned in a dream that King Herod wanted to murder the infant. The family then fled to Egypt;
- On hearing of the death of Herod in 4 BCE, the family returned to Nazareth;
- When Jesus was 12 years of age, Mary and Joseph took him to a Passover celebration in Jerusalem. Returning home, they were separated from Jesus thinking he was with others. Frantically, they searched for him, finding him in the Temple among religious elders.
- Mary virtually becomes invisible. She is at a wedding feast at Cana where she encouraged Jesus to help solve the shortage of wine. On another occasion, Mary and extended family members request that Jesus be alerted to them. He reminds the crowd that his brothers and sisters are those who hear God's word and keep it.

- Mary is found at the foot of the cross of Jesus' crucifixion along with John. Mary Magdalene and Mary pf Cleopas.
- After the ascension of Jesus, Mary and other women are members of the apostles in Jerusalem waiting for the Holy Spirit to strengthen them.
- Mary is alleged to have lived for 11 years after Jesus' ascension into heaven. According to Catholic tradition, on her death (41 CE), she was taken to heaven body and soul.

We had our third cooking class this evening with a full house of participants including Ed Malone. The word is out that these classes are special. It was moved to Tuesday because scheduling conflicts. The theme was Indian cooking or as they also are known as curries. Jerome led this class, explaining all the traditional herbs used in curries, including samples of vegetable pakoras, tandoori chicken, Basa fish tikka, Aloo Gobi (vegetables), naan bread and the coconut flavored basmati rice. The aromas were enough by themselves. Our teachers were given a long warm applause at the end of the evening.

Father in heaven, thank you for all the good things in my life that give such pleasure, especially the teaching on Mary and the Samaritan Club's Indian cooking class today.

# Wednesday, December 15,
# Joint meeting of the Pastoral Council,
# the CWA and the Men's Club

Mantra for the Day:

"The Lord is gracious and merciful, slow to anger and abounding in steadfast love. The Lord is good to all, and his compassion is over all that he has made." (Book of Psalms, ch. 145, v. 8-9)

I emailed the members of the interdenominational group explaining the Bishop Ben has been promoted and an experienced older priest, Father Mike and I will be called to administer the Diocese until a new Bishop is announced. I will be away in early January joining my family in San Diego for six days. We will be resuming our monthly meetings in February.

I prepared a special parish bulletin announcing the Christmas season of St Francis/St. Brigid/St Joseph's Christmas services. I will ask Ed to publish it in the Prairie News too.

> Confessions: St. Francis Thursday, December 23, 5:00 to 6:00 pm and 7:00 to 9:00 pm; Friday, December 24, 3:00 to 4:00 pm;
>
> Christmas Eve Anglican Liturgical Service, December 24, 5:00 pm to 7:00 pm; Christmas Eve Catholic Mass, December 24, 7:30 pm;
>
> Christmas Day Mass, December 25, 10:00 am at St. Francis' Church and noon at St. Joseph's Church.
>
> Christmas Day Anglican Liturgical Service, December 25, 5:00 pm to 7:00 pm at St. Francis.
>
> There will be NO Sunday Catholic Masses or Anglican Liturgical Services at St Francis and St Joseph's on December 26 this year.
>
> New Year's Day Catholic Mass at 10:00 am in St. Francis and Noon in St. Joseph's.
>
> There will be an Anglican Liturgical Services on January 01 this year at St. Francis at 5:00 pm.

I emailed this tentative schedule to Claire for her approval. She replied immediately, agreed and thanked me. I emailed it to Ed Malone for inclusion in the next edition of the Prairie News.

That evening, we had meeting of the CWA, the Pastoral Council and the Men's Club. I informed them about Bishop Ben's promotion to Quebec City. Someone chipped in, will he still cheer for Edmonton's football and hockey teams? Father Mike and I will jointly administer the Diocese until the Vatican announces a replacement. Unfortunately, Father Mike's has severe heart problems and consequently, I will be expected to carry most of the load. I expect to remain at St. Francis indefinitely with all of you. The only difference is that I will be absent from the parish from time to time managing diocesan responsibilities and I will be expected to travel to Bishop's meetings occasionally. I informed them that Margaret, his secretary will be staying on during this transition. An informal "come and go" event at the Cathedral on Wednesday, December 29, between 7:00 pm and 9:00 pm for those wishing to say good bye. We are entering a busy time in the Church's liturgical calendar with Christmas and New Years when Catholics make their twice-annual trip to Church. In early January, I will join my family in San Diego for six days. They have rented a big house for January to get my parents out of this cold climate.

To my question about having the Anglicans sharing our Church, a number of people responded favourably. Bill said that he experienced the Anglican mass in a whole different way, much more communal, a friendlier way of being at Church. Ned said that they seemed more relaxed. Mabel thought that having a meal begin the service brought everyone together. When I asked them if we should consider doing that ourselves, they agreed.

Bill reported that a total of ten men and two women have begun snow shovelling and caring for the two outdoor skating rinks. They start at 7:00 am and work for an hour. They are getting terrific feedback. Three members are high school students. Residents are phoning the Town Office thanking them for this new service. The Town Office is acknowledging that this is an initiative of St. Francis.

Father in heaven, thank you again for your many blessings. Thank you for Claire and the Anglicans, Margaret, the Bishop's secretary, the CWA, the Men's Club and the Parish Council who are so accommodating. Thank you for Ed Malone and the use of his weekly newspaper to deliver our news. I hope you will guide Father Raj, Susan and Maggie as they make life-changing decisions. Please continue to care for Father Ryan, the homeless, the sick, and the dying. Thank you.

## Thursday, December 16
## A quiet day of office work

> Mantra for the Day:
>
> "I sought the Lord and he answered me, and delivered me from all my fears. This poor soul cried, and was heard by the Lord, and was saved from every trouble" (Book of Psalms, ch. 34, v. 4-6).

Jerome emailed me asking for Tuesday, December 28 at 10:00 am for their wedding. I agreed. Yes, they wanted a complete mass with the Eucharist. Good.

Ed phoned asking for an invite for coffee tomorrow morning. He will bring Tim Horton's coffee and some blueberry muffins. Yes, please come.

I had a quiet day catching up with diocesan paper work given to me by Margaret last week. Lots of reading.

Father in heaven, thank you for this opportunity to serve you and those whom you love.

# Friday, December 17
# Ed Malone arrives with muffins and coffee

My mantra for the day:

"I will sing of your steadfast love, O Lord, forever; with my mouth I will proclaim your faithfulness to all generations. I declare that your steadfast love is established forever; your faithfulness is as firm as the heavens" (Book of Psalms, ch. 89, v. 1-2).

Sis emailed me telling me that the whole family would be joining us for the community Christmas dinner. I emailed Ed that there would ten Walkers joining us for dinner on Tuesday.

10:00 am Ed Malone arrived with two large Timmies' coffees and two blueberry muffins (my weakness, blueberry muffins). He was all business, a search and confirm suspicion assignment with tape recorder in hand. He asked if Mabel has been in touch with me. Yes, she has. I reminded him that she, along with Claire and Joan are heading up the Developing Nations Aid Program. He continued that he has had two meeting with her about a class action suit against the Canadian Catholic Church and its discriminatory attitude towards women. He wanted to know what my role was in all this. A question right out of the Cardinal's mouth. I explained that she and I had coffee at Tim's where she laid these plans out. She wanted to know if I knew a good Catholic lawyer and I suggested Paul Taylor. He continued that she was planning a cross Canada tour to get the support of Catholic Women Association's members, (a national Catholic women's organization). Paul thinks that if the group takes the Canadian Catholic Church as a whole to court, meaning all the dioceses in Canada, they can go straight to the Supreme

Court of Canada for a quicker decision. (Ed has a best seller in the back of his mind. I am getting good at reading his mind). Ed continued that Mabel had even asked him if he would like to travel with her on her "crusade". The Tribune was considering paying both Mabel's and his expenses (Such a good business decision).

After an unusual uncomfortable silence, he asked me how I felt about her initiative. I said that I will reply if it is "off the record". He turned off his recorder to give me his assurance. Carefully choosing my words, I said that Mabel and Ned were a real power couple. They are a driving force in the parish and I love and admire them. But I would not want to be on her bad side. On the other hand, I was in favour of whatever made the Church more attractive and welcoming to people. I asked him when he and Mabel were leaving? He said probably next week if the newspaper came through with his expenses. I asked him if this subject would really sell papers? Yes. It really would. The discrimination of women by an organization like the Catholic Church is hot news.

I spent the rest of the day preparing the biblical background for the information sheets of marriage, baptism, confirmation and the sacrament for the sick. These will be utilized in the new Deaconate program.

Father in heaven, I continue to thank you for your love and kindness towards me, your St. Francis/St. Joseph families, your Anglican families, my family, friends and especially Mabel and Ed.

# Saturday/Sunday, December 18/19
# Preach "Mary, the mother of Jesus"

> "All who heard it were amazed by what had been told them by the shepherds. And Mary kept all these things, reflecting on them in her heart" (Gospel of Luke, ch. 2, v. 18-19).

I emailed Margaret requesting her to organize a short meeting of key members of the key Diocesan organizations especially the finance committee and the pastoral council. The subject was to be diocesan finances and paying of our new debt resulting from the Father Ryan court case. She replied that she was on it (she amazes me with her responsiveness).

I received an email from Maggie requesting my presence at a family meeting scheduled for tomorrow, Monday at 10:00 am at the family home. I responded in the affirmative.

I preached about "Mary, the mother of Jesus"

> *"Dear friends, thank you for coming to Mass today and including God our loving Father in your day. I wish to chat with you about Mary's vocation as the mother of Jesus, a very important role in the life of the Church for a number of reasons. She is an exemplary role model on Christian behavior. You will recall that artists have depicted her at prayer when the Angel Gabriel appeared to her inviting her to become the mother of Jesus. Gabriel calls her a favored person of God. She is told that she will become pregnant with a son, whose name is to be Jesus, the son of God. Remember, that at the time she was only betrothed to marry Joseph, but the marriage ceremony had not been completed. She was still living at home. Obviously, this invitation would have been*

*very bewildering to her. Being pregnant and not married would have been dangerous as Mary could have been stoned to death in accordance with Jewish law at the time.*

*Imagine that for the first 22 weeks of Mary's pregnancy with Jesus, when medical science doubts if a fetus can survive on its own, she (in her body) would have been his exclusive source of life. How extraordinary and challenging to fathom?*

*It was at this time that another extraordinary event was occurring. Her cousin Elizabeth was pregnant in her old age. She and her husband Zachariah were to become the parents of John the Baptist. Their stories were similar in some ways.*

*The back story is that while Zachariah was performing his priestly duties in the temple, the Angel Gabriel appeared to him. Gabriel reassuringly stated that their prayers for a child had been heard by God. Elizabeth was to give birth to a son, John the Baptist who was to be a public relations person to Jesus. Zachariah was incredulous; how can two old people have a child? Gabriel replied because you won't believe me, you will not be able to speak until your son John is circumcised. Zachariah eventually got his voice back when he confirmed that the boy should be called John at his circumcision.*

*Now Mary, was caught off guard by this visit of Angel Gabriel. The angel told her that her cousin Elizabeth was six months pregnant, in spite of being well past a child bearing age. Nothing is impossible with God. Mary consented to become the mother of Jesus and agreed to do whatever*

*God wanted. Mary, while not understanding the details, trusted God to lead the way and she would follow.*

*How often are we asked to either do things or accommodate something totally unexpected? Probably more than we realize. However, it is in these moments that we turn our thoughts to God, asking for guidance in both understanding and confidence to allow these unusual events to occur.*

*The Gospel of Luke in three events presents Mary as being both a calm and receptive person. Luke states that while Mary was perplexed by the Angel's greeting, "Hail full of grace", the angel was very reassuring and that she had nothing to fear. God the father was inviting her to become the mother of Jesus and she only needed to consent. Mary consented.*

*At the birth of Jesus in Bethlehem, the family, Joseph, Mary and Jesus were visited by shepherds who explained that an angel had appeared to them announcing with great joy the birth of the long-awaited messiah. Mary kept all these things, reflecting on them in her heart. Again, she was a calm and reflective person.*

*Some years later during the feast of the Passover in Jerusalem, Jesus inadvertently remained in the city, while his parents retuned home thinking he was included in the returning caravan. After realizing that he was not, they anxiously began searching for him. After three days, they found him in the Temple talking to a group of teachers. Jesus, however, did not seem to even acknowledge or apologize for the worry he had caused Mary and Joseph. Luke seemed to imply that one's spiritual development exceeded family relationships. Again, Mary kept all these things in her heart.*

*Mary's behavior is a role model at the marriage feast of Cana and in her silent support of Jesus on the cross. At Cana, for some unexpected reason, the wedding planner did not anticipate the amount of wine needed for this wedding. Sensing the potential embarrassment to the families and the organizers, Mary asks Jesus to help solve the problem. He responds, by asking her why this matter is of concern. His time for work had not yet begun. But Mary persisted and Jesus performed a miracle changing water into wine for the occasion.*

*At Jesus' suffering and death on the cross, Mary silently has accompanied him on this deathly journey. Standing at the foot of the cross, she, accompanied by Mary the wife of Cleopas, Mary Magdalene and John, the apostle, carried out this vigil until he died. Before He died, he asked John to look after His mother. She demonstrates courage, loyalty and strength.*

*At the end of her life on earth, she is believed to have been taken to heaven body and soul. Mary is a wonderful role model for us."*

## Dinner with family

The Christmas hype was in full force at dinner. The four grandchildren were very excited about the beautifully decorated tree in my parent's living room and all the gifts under it. While there was not supposed to be any touching or shaking of the gifts by the four of them, it was hard to encourage them to sit quietly and have our dinner. I excused myself before dessert, wished them all a Merry Christmas and said that I would be back next Sunday for Christmas dinner. Mother normally put on a special spread at Christmas.

Father in heaven thank you for a special day including preaching about Mary. Guide us to keep a balance in purchasing gifts for family and friends and carrying for the poor and homeless at this special time.

## Monday, December 20
## Meeting the Taylor family and
## Maggie's pregnancy

Mantra for the Day:

"Are not two sparrows sold for a small coin? Yet no one of them falls to the ground without your Father's knowledge. Even the hairs of your head are counted. So, do not be afraid; you are worth more than many sparrows"
(Gospel of Matthew, ch. 3, v. 13-14).

9:00 am, I emailed Margaret to see if there were any glitches in the farewell plans for the Bishop. She assured me that things were progressing as planned.

At precisely 10:00 am. I arrived at Paul and Simone's home. Paul politely welcomed me into the living room of their gracious home. After coffee was served, Maggie held up her hands for silence and began her story. She had been to a graduation party in a park out of town. It was rowdy with drinking and goofing off. She was offered what she vaguely recalls as a Quaalude. She remembers waking up without her underwear and feeling very unclean. When she asked her friends about it, they too were hazy about what happened. She was the only woman there who had become pregnant. She explained that she had talked to me on two occasions about the pros and cons of both keeping the baby and having an abortion. She had a gynecologist confirm that she was actually pregnant. While attending Law School at McGill University, she was able to board with a small group of nuns, the Sisters of Charity, that provide social services in the low-income neighbourhoods of Montreal. The Sisters were very supportive and understanding. Dad, as you can probably imagine, Law School took over my life especially since I was a late entry. I was not feeling very sociable anyway. After a time, I felt that I had a personal companion in this big lonely city. At that point, I decided against having an abortion.

Paul jumped in saying that carrying this by yourself must have been frightening, but asked why did she not go to the police? She said three reasons: total embarrassment and humiliation over my horrible mistake, fear of shaming you and Mom and I did not want to burden you with this problem.

Simone expressed her surprise and her disappointment that Maggie did not try to confide in her. She replied to her that she was frightened and ashamed.

Paul looked at me and asked if I had anything to add. I said no, I am only here to listen and be supportive. I did say that I truly admire Maggie's courage and maturity. She has demonstrated a level of confidence well beyond her years.

As the conversation wound down and sensing that all this information needed to processed by the family, I excused myself but offered to come back if requested. Paul showed me to the door. I thanked him for all his work on behalf of Father Ryan. Paul's parting remarks were that your Bishop made some very strategic interventions which helped to sway Judge Harrison. He thanked me for referring Mabel to him. Paul continued, asking when he could talk to me about this unusual and awkward class action suit and he have his secretary phone me to set up a meeting. I agreed.

Claire emailed that the Christmas notice in the newspaper should include both Church names. Agreed, I replied. St Francis/St. Brigid/St. Joseph had a nice ring to it.

I phoned Father Mike suggesting that since we are losing Father Hildebrand to cancer, Father Ryan to prison and Father Raj to a leave of absence, we desperately need reinforcements, would you please accompany me to visit the Abbot at the Benedictine Monastery to request some help? He agreed. We agreed to leave Wednesday morning early. I phoned Father Joe explaining the nature of our visit. He invited us and thanked me for the heads up.

Monday afternoon, I received my sixteen-pound turkey with the instructions to have it cooked and delivered to the school gym by 5:00 pm Tuesday.

Father in heaven, thank you for today. Thank you for the opportunity to be a fly on the wall of the Taylor's family meeting this morning, for Father Mike, for Father Joe and for the turkey.

## Tuesday, December 21
## Cooking the big bird

Mantra for the Day:

"Whatever you ask the Father in my name, He will give it to you. Until now You have not asked anything in my name; ask and you will receive" (Gospel, of John, ch. 16, v. 23-24).

Tuesday's correspondence scripture studies were cancelled until mid-January.

At 10:00 am, I began to prepare the turkey for roasting. Mother estimated that it would take 5.5 hours to roast unstuffed at 350 degrees uncovered. Basting was required every 30 minutes. I spent the day in the kitchen and then to the school gym.

At 5:00 pm I welcomed my family into the rectory and gave them the grand tour of the Church and rectory. Their first visit except for Mother's visits. We had our own table in the gym. I introduced my parents, my siblings and my nieces and nephews who were given a roaring round of applause. There were 650 plates of turkey and trimmings served. The books for each child including my nieces and nephews, were a big success. The Mayor opened the evening and thanked everyone for their contribution. Lots of applause. What a great event.

Ed emailed to say that the Tribune had decided not to fund his participation in Mabel's "crusade." He was not disappointed as he felt that he was abandoning Elaine. I replied inquiring if the Cardinal had anything to do with the Tribune's decision. He replied, possibly. How much does the Cardinal know about Mabel's crusade? Silence.

Father in heaven, thank you for another special day of pastoral work, the community Christmas dinner and of course my family.

## Wednesday, December 22
## The Trip to the Monastery

Mantra for the Day:

"If you remain in me and my words remain in you, ask for whatever you want and it will be done for you" (Gospel of John, ch. 15, v. 7).

The 3-hour car ride to the monastery was very pleasant. Father Mike talked all the way there about growing up on a farm and how much he missed rural life. It was so much simpler than urban living. Finally, I asked him if he would like a change to a small-town parish. He did not answer. I asked further if St. Francis would interest him. He was adamant that such a move would be going from the frying pan into the fire. We were welcomed at the monastery by Father Joe. After a brief stop in the chapel, we headed to the refectory. We were welcomed to the Abbot's table. Lunch was chicken noodle soup, fresh bread and cheese (I just love the healthy wholesome food here). After lunch, the Abbot arose and invited all the monks to join him for a special meeting in the refectory. He introduced us and sat down, asking me to lead the discussion. I thanked them all again for their wonderful hospitality. I then explained the background to our staffing problems. Father Hildebrand has serious terminal cancer, Father Ryan is now in permanent custody, Father Raj has married and looking for work with the Anglican Church. We need three or four priests to assist us on weekends. There would be some weekday work as well, but it is not defined as yet. We would happily cover their expenses. A question and answer period followed fleshing out the details. I then thanked them for taking in Father Ryan. He is the sole person in the guest suite and seems to be settling in. The Abbot then updated everyone on the development of special penitentiary quarters at the monastery that is moving forward. We tried to visit Father Ryan, but he refused. Our return to the city was uneventful. Father Mike slept most of the way. He agreed to contact neighboring priests, requesting them to please fill in for the parishes without priests. Apologize to them as this season is the wrong time to be taking on other responsibilities. Alert them that help in on the way in early January.

Margaret emailed that a special meeting has been organized for Monday, 7:00 pm, January 03. There will only be eight members present but they are key members. Thank you, Margaret.

Father in heaven, thank you for Father Mike, the Benedictines, Margaret, and Father Ryan in my life. Working with them is like having lessons in how to love. They gently but clearly expand my boundaries.

# Thursday, December 23
# More on the Taylors and Father Raj.

> Mantra for the Day:
>
> "I am the true vine, and my Father is the vine grower. He takes away every branch in me that does not bear fruit, and everyone that does, he prunes so that it bears more fruit" (Gospel of John, ch. 15, v. 1-2).

I phoned Simone to inquire how they were doing. She said that they are still shocked, upset and unsure what to do. They have decided to have a very quiet Christmas and to pray for guidance. They are going to Mass and reconnecting as a family in a very quiet way. I asked about Maggie. Simone replied that she seems unusually serene given her circumstances. She thanked me for calling and for spending time with Maggie.

I received an email from Father Raj. advising me that he would be spending Christmas with Masala and wished me heartfelt blessings of the Lord at this special time.

Father in heaven, thank you for another day working with you. The Taylors seem to be managing well with their new addition to the family. Father Raj. is working out his future with Masala. Please keep them all in your love and embrace. Thank you.

## Friday/Saturday December 24/25
## Christmas:

Mantra for the Day:

"Glory to God in the highest. Peace on earth to all women and men who love Him" (Gospel of Luke, ch. 2, v. 13-14).

## I preached "How Christ changed the world"

*"My dear friends, this is my first Christmas with you. Thank you for making my life so rich in love and experiences. I wish also to thank our Anglican brother and sisters for setting up the creche in the Church. I want to welcome those of you visiting St. Francis parish. Thank you for coming. We have coffee and cookies after Mass in the rectory boardroom for those of you who have time. Please join us.*

*The birth of Jesus was truly a game-changing event. Jesus, the second person of the Blessed Trinity and the most powerful being in the world, allowed himself to become a vulnerable infant. God's presented himself in many different ways in his interactions with our ancestors as outlined in the Old Testament. We are told in Genesis, the first book of the Bible, that God created us in His image and His likeness. He walked in the Garden of Eden with Adam and Eve, our first parents. Abraham saw God with two angels. Angels were common communicators or companions. Moses encountered God in a burning bush that did not consume the bush. But now, Jesus changed the way we look at each other. Christmas reminds us that we can never look at an infant again without wondering if this is another Jesus. We can see Jesus or goodness in those around us. Jesus worked, he partied, he wept, he became angry and changed our humanity by showing us how to live. He still used His divine power to knock St Paul off his horse for persecuting the early Christians. Jesus reminded Paul that when he persecuted Christians, he was persecuting him. Jesus identified himself with us. Jesus showed us what being a son or daughter entailed.*

*Merry Christmas everyone."*

## Christmas dinner with family

Dinner with the family especially at Christmas is mayhem at best. Lots of noise, excitement, food, drink and hockey. It was great not to be talking about my issues. I got home early and watched some old recorded NFL games on TV.

There were twenty-five emails wishing me the best of the season. It will take a few days to reply to them.

Father in heaven, thank you again for all you do for me, my family, my parishioners, my friends, especially Jerome and Raymond.

# Monday, December 27
# Farewells for Bishop Ben

Mantra for the Day:

"Now, Master, you may let your servant go in peace, according to your word. My eyes have seen your salvation, which you prepared in the sight of all peoples; A light for revelation to the Gentiles and glory for your people Israel" (Gospel of Luke, ch. 2, v. 29-32).

## Priest's good-bye lunch for Bishop Ben

The Christmas spirit prevailed over this event. There must have been about twenty-five priests present. There was lots of laughter and kibitzing around, typical of priest get-togethers. Bishop Ben spoke, thanking everyone for coming on such a cold day. It was a -18 degrees C. I suspected that some of the out-of- towners would have said good-bye earlier or phoned him. He apologized for leaving many things unfinished, but he was assured that both Fathers Mike and Cam would clean up any messes he left incomplete. Margaret has agreed to stay on during this transition.

Ed and Elaine brought pizza and wine for a late dinner. Elaine told us about what it was like having Father Ryan in their secured facility. He did not have much to say but was always very polite to hospital staff. He was very tidy. He regularly asked Constable Melanie Campbell to play cribbage with him. A mystery man.

I heard that the Come and Go in the evening was very pleasant. Mabel and Ned from the parish attended as did Fred and Thelma. They emailed me the details and reported that many expressed sadness at the Bishop's departure.

Father in heaven, thank you for such a fun day. I pray for the Pope, the Bishops, the priests, the Margarets, the Father Ryans, Ed and Elaine. Keep them in your care.

## Tuesday, December 28
## Jerome's and Raymond's wedding

Mantra for the Day:

"Listening to the Lord is the beginning of wisdom, and the knowledge of God is insight. For by me your days will be multiplied and years will be added to your life" (Book of Proverbs, ch. 9, v. 10-11).

Jerome and Raymond's wedding was very special. As promised, there were only fourteen family members in attendance. Jerome read a text from the First Letter of John about love; where there is love, God is present as God is the source of love. Raymond read a text from Paul's First Letter to the Corinthians where love is described as patient and kind. Then they shared examples of their love that makes their lives unique and special. At the end of their words, we all clapped for them and gave them a long warm hug. The music was wonderful and the rest of the Mass was beautiful.

After lunch Ed Malone and I had a short meeting. I asked him to become my new communications director. He quickly agreed. I told him that I needed his services for sixteen hours or two days a week. I also reminded him that his communications with Cardinal George concerning matters of this Diocese, whether emails, telephone conversations, and even letters had to be approved by me first. He looked at me long and hard as if to say that it was contrary to his professional ethics. I reminded him that even he has an editor at the Tribune who does that before his submissions are approved for print. He finally acquiesced. We closed our visit agreeing to an hourly rate of $100.00 per hour. He was delighted. After he left, I realized that Ed will eventually get an interesting book out of this experience.

Father in heaven, thank you for all that you do for me. Thank you for being born in Canada and for giving me such a good life. Thank you for Jerome and Raymond and their LGBTQIA+ community. They are models of kindness and gentleness. Thank you for Ed and Elaine. I will need to keep a close reign on his communications with the Cardinal. I pray for the Pope, the Bishops, the priests of the diocese, my parishioners, my family, the lonely, the depressed, sick family and friends and finally the dying.

## Wednesday, December 29
## Funeral for Conrad, Marion's former husband

> Mantra for the Day:
>
> "Out of the depths I cry to you, O Lord. Lord, hear my voice! If you, O Lord, should mark iniquities, who could stand? But there is forgiveness with you. For with the Lord there is steadfast love" (Book of Psalms, ch. 130, v. 1-4).

At 10:00 am, the funeral of Marion's ex-husband Conrad was held in the parish. He had been cremated in Vancouver. In addition to Colin and Marion, there was a small group from St. Francis such as Fred and Thelma, Ned (Mabel was still on her CWA tour), Bill and Liz McMillan, Tom and Ann McCaffrey, Jim and Judy Truman and Mario and Isabella Demarco and their children.

Colin read the short text of St. Dismas, the good thief, who was crucified with Jesus. As he was dying on the cross, he asked Jesus to forgive his mistakes. Jesus gave him his assurances that upon his death, he would be taken immediately to heaven. Marion read the story of the Prodigal Son who after leading desolate life, spending his inheritance, was still welcomed back into the family by his father. These stories quietly expressed their thoughts and feelings about Conrad. I was reminded that even though Colin and Marion were married, they would never get their previous marriages annulled. Should I be checking if they are legally married? Why would it matter if they were not? Their story would help in the debate about divorced people receiving the Eucharist. The funeral was concluded with a small reception in the parish hall.

Father in heaven, thank you for this special day. Thank you for the kind people of this parish, Colin, Marion and the members of the parish who took the time to attend this funeral.

## Thursday, December 30
## The Benedictines have agreed to help

Mantra for the Day:

"Lord, you are tender, full of love and forgiving, abounding in steadfast love to all who call upon you" (Book of Psalms, ch. 86, v. 5).

I emailed Margaret asking her to please invite all the priests in the diocese for a short one-hour meeting scheduled for 10:00 am Monday morning, January 03 at the Cathedral boardroom.

Father Joe called to say that he and his Benedictine colleagues were ready to join us and help out. I asked them to arrive on January 02 during the day. We would meet at Father Mike's Parish where he will put you up until we can your accommodation sorted out. Your new accommodation in the city will be Bishop Ben's former apartment. Father Mike and Margaret will help you and your colleagues get established and get your apartment ready for you. On Monday, we would like your group to join a meeting of all the priests in the diocese at the Cathedral boardroom at 10:00 am.

Father in heaven, thank you for Father Joe and the "Bennies" and for a quiet day today permitting me to watch an NFL game between the Patriots and the Chiefs.

## Friday, December 31
## Catch Up Day and Dinner with Parents

Mantra for the Day:

"I will give thanks to the Lord with my whole heart; I will tell of all your wondrous deeds" (Book of Psalms, ch. 9, v. 1).

A quiet day that afforded me to catch up on my readings. I now have to read what is happening in all the other parishes in the diocese.

I drove to the City to have a quiet dinner with my parents as they will be away for the month of January in San Diego. I got their permission to sleep in my own bed when I work late in the city. They wholeheartedly agreed. We did not discuss my work.

Father in heaven, thank you for my parents. Please watch over them and all the other people I pray for.

# CHAPTER 3

# *Journal Entries for January*

## Saturday/Sunday, January 01/02
## Preach "Have I told you lately that I love you?"

Mantra for the Day:

"Love never gives up. Love cares more for others than for self. Love doesn't want what it does not have. Love does not strut, doesn't have a swelled head, doesn't force itself on others, isn't always "me first," doesn't fly off the handle, does not keep score of the sins of others, doesn't revel when others grovel, takes pleasure in the truth, puts up with anything, trusts God always, always looks for the best, never looks back, but keeps going to the end" (First Letter of Paul to the Corinthians, ch. 13, v. 4-7).

*"My dear friends, as we begin a new year, I thought it might be suitable for a small change in my weekly chats with you. I recently heard the song titled 'Have I told you recently that I love*

*you?' I won't sing it for you now and embarrass myself. I will admit however, that my singing voice is much better when I am in the shower or alone in my car. This song has been made famous and popular for years by many well-known vocalists, including Gene Autry, Bing Crosby, Elvis Presley, Jim Reeves, Ray Price, Van Morrison and Rod Stewart. Two verses of the song go like this:*

*'Have I told you lately that I love you? Have I told you there is no one above you? You fill my heart with gladness, take away my sadness, ease my troubles, that is what you do.*

*For the morning sun and all its glory greets the day with hope and comfort too. You fill my life with laughter and somehow you make it better, ease my troubles, that is what you do.*

*There is a love that is divine, and it's yours and it's mine, like the sun at the end of the day, we should give thanks and pray to the one."*

*Some people make resolutions at the beginning of a new year. These can include lose weight, exercise more, eat more wholesome foods and take an evening class. I am recommending that you express your love for one another more frequently this year especially to your partner and to your children. I recommend telling them every day that you love them. Use this song as a reminder to tell the special people in your life, you wife, your husband and yes, even you children that you love them. It makes them feel good.*

*There is also a spiritual component to this song. Van Morrison acknowledged such in his life. Thanking God, our loving father in heaven, for all the good things we have in our lives is important too. It acknowledges that God has given us everything, our lives, our health, life in Canada, our partner in marriage, our children, our family, and our friends. Just as it is important to recognize the joy, happiness and well-being our partner gives us, so, it is also important to recognize and acknowledge all the blessings that we receive from God our loving father in heaven.*

*Normally, we begin each new year with resolutions. I have a few for you to consider: first, dedicate your day to the Father in heaven and pray for guidance, wisdom and patience in dealing with the many people and issues that can unfold; second, at lunch, find a few moments to check into how you are doing and resolve to do better; and finally, at the end of your day, review how you did, ask for forgiveness where you failed and thank the Father for His many gifts. So, the next time you hear this song playing, you can thank our Father in heaven, your partner and your children for their love and care for you."*

Father in heaven, again a special thank you. Help me not to take you for granted. I love you.

## Monday, January 03
## A meeting of the Diocesan priests and the Diocesan Finance Committee

Mantra for the Day:

"Create in me a clean heart, O God, and put a new and right spirit within me. Do not cast me away from your presence and do not take your holy spirit from me" (Book of Psalms, ch. 51, v. 10-11).

At 10:00 am, Father Mike and I called the meeting to order. I thanked the priests for coming especially on such a cold winter day. The temperature was -16 degrees Celsius. I introduced Ed Malone to them, as our new Diocesan communications director. I explained his role was to keep you, your parishes and the community at large informed of our Church plans for the future. We will not be sitting on our hands waiting for the appointment of a new Bishop.

I updated them on the Father Ryan affair, the marriage of Father Raj and severe health problems of Father Hildebrand, the three new Benedictine temporary replacements (Fathers Joe, Leo and Peter), the state of our finances and the anticipated long wait for a new Bishop. They listened calmly, asked a ton of questions that Ed and I quickly wrote down as the subject of a future Diocesan newsletter. I informed them that there would be other similar meetings in the months to come focussing on the needs of priests. The meeting ended with an Italian bean soup, Italian deli meat sandwiches and black coffee. They will be wide awake driving home.

At 5:30 pm, Father Mike and I had an early dinner. We chatted quietly about the upcoming meeting at 7:00 pm.

At 7:00 pm, a small group of both men and women met with Father Mike and I to discuss diocesan finances in the Cathedral boardroom. According to Charles Dobson, the chairman of the finance committee, the Father Ryan court case put us nearly a million dollar in debt. Apart from this debt, the diocesan finances were in a manageable state with the exception of the recent church and rectory fire. When we asked to consider our alternatives. Charles indicated that there were three alternatives including a special tithe of 10% of every parishioner, a diocesan lottery and selling some church property. The finance committee would evaluate these alternatives and make a recommendation. He also added that the Court wants to charge the diocese a 5% interest on unpaid balances. The worst case would be $45,000.00 a year in interest payments or a daily penalty of $123.28. I drove Father Mike back to his rectory in silence. As he left the car, I assured him that I would consult Paul Taylor about an appeal and talk to Charles about other options. He thanked me for the ride and complained of chest pains. I asked him if I could drive him to the hospital, but he assured me that he had some nitroglycerine tablets that usually worked with this type of pain.

I emailed Paul explaining our financial situation and asked his opinion of the value of an appeal? I emailed Charles Dobson asking him for his opinion on what was the best option for paying off these court costs and avoiding interest charges.

Father in heaven, thank you for my priest colleagues and the finance committee members. They are very gracious and kind.

## January 04 to 09
## Tuesday to Saturday, San Diego

> Mantra for the Day:
>
> "Our Father, who are in heaven, hallowed be your name. Bring your plan for heaven and earth to fruition. Keep giving us the things we need to serve you and our fellow human beings. Keep forgiving us as we continue to forgive others" (Gospel of Matthew, ch. 6, v. 9-12).

My sister drove me to the local airport as brother and his family would be hosting the first two weeks. Fortunately, she had both her children in the car thus preventing her from giving me a bad time as she usually does. I flew with WestJet to San Diego for a long overdue holiday. My brother met me at the airport and drove me to what the family was now calling the Walker's "Hilton Hotel" for the month of January. I spent the afternoon in the pool with my nephew and niece. Brother barbequed some turkey burgers for dinner. I have a bedroom with attached bathroom in the basement. I love it here. It is like living in a cave.

On Wednesday, Paul Taylor emailed saying that an appeal was definitely possible but a different judge may decide to adjudicate a tougher sentence for Father Ryan and could increase the financial compensation. There would be more legal fees and court costs. The existing court decision was a good package deal and, in his opinion, not worth challenging.

Charles emailed with bad news. In reviewing the options under consideration, the lottery option is not recommended as it would take a year to get organized and operating and would not make a profit until after the second year. The Committee does not think that a tithe of 10% would not receive an acceptable reception in the diocese given the nature of Father Ryan's offence. Selling some Church property seems to be the best option. Selling rural or small-town parish properties, however, would not generate the amount of money needed. The best property would be the Cathedral and that is because of its location and its land value. He concluded by asking how I felt about renting space say at the Anglican Cathedral Church down the street?

The family organized a tour of the Zoo, a water park with long water slides before heading for our rental home for dinner and pool time. I, particularly enjoyed the water slides with my niece and nephew. Young children can be the source of great fun.

I found a quiet time with my father and my brother Paul to explain the diocesan finances, hoping for some fresh suggestions. I also told them that Father Raj was probably leaving to get married, if he is not already married to his high school classmate from India. They agreed with Charles' suggestion to sell the Cathedral and rent space from the nearby

Anglican Cathedral. They also suggested to pursue the lottery idea as a long-term goal.

I emailed Ed asking him to prepare a draft Diocesan newsletter for my review. He should answer all the questions left unanswered at the priests meeting, talk about our aging priesthood and the critical nature of our diocesan finances. Finally, it should include the development of a Diocesan plan. He replied if he should be writing something on Mabel's class action suit? I replied, not yet.

Thursday and Friday zipped by with leisurely breakfasts at the pool, trips to the beach and goofing around family time. My parents seemed relaxed and loved the family time together.

Father in heaven, what are your thoughts? Will it be the end of the world if the Diocese does not have a Cathedral Church for a period of time? Thank you for my family.

## Saturday/Sunday, January 09/10
## Preach "Praying like Abraham"

> Mantra for the Day:
>
> "Now the Lord told Abram (later renamed Abraham) 'leave your country and your family and your father's home for a land that I will show you. I will make you a great nation and bless you. I will make your name famous, you will be a blessing. I will bless those who bless you and those who curse you, I will curse; and all the families of the earth shall be blessed through you. So, Abram left just as God said'"(Book of Genesis, ch. 12, v. 1-4)

Back to reality; my brother drove me back to the airport on Saturday morning. My return flight on WestJet was uneventful.

Sis met me at the airport with a warm winter coat, tuque and gloves. We had some lunch before I returned to St. Francis for my normal weekend duties. Western Canada was in a deep freeze. Yuk!!!

## Preach "Praying like Abraham"

> "Dear friends, your -18 degrees Celsius weather is a challenge after spending a few days with my family in San Diego, California.
> My subject today is praying with Abraham. Jesus recommended that we are to pray always. I would like to share with you my understanding of Abraham's prayer life. Abraham was a man of prayer. Abraham was known for listening to God and following God's instructions and wishes. In Genesis, the first book of the Old Testament, Abraham is asked by God to leave his country, thought to be modern day Turkey and move his family, his herds and flocks to Canaan, to what is today known as Israel where he will become the father of a great nation. He was seventy-five years old at the time and Sarai his wife was barren. God promises Abraham that he will become the father of a great nation. Abraham obeys God's request and takes his nephew Lot with him. Upon arriving in Canaan, Abraham builds an altar and worships God. Soon time passes and God and two angels appear at Abram's tent in the desert on a very hot day. Abraham follows the hospitality rules of the day and provides refreshments water, food and rest. During this visit God explains to Abraham that he has heard bad things about Sodom and Gomorrah, a city nearby where his nephew Lot

*lived with his family. God advises him that he is about to destroy these cities. Abraham begins to persuade God to change his mind. He asks God if He would consider not destroying it if there are fifty good people living in it. God replies, yes. Calling on God's goodness and wisdom, Abraham then asks God if He would consider saving it if there were just forty good people. Again, God agrees. This dialogue continues with Abraham cajoling or even begging God to be merciful and kind to the two cities if there were only forty good people, then thirty, then twenty and finally only ten. God eventually agrees. Persistence is a key to our prayer.*

*God tells Abraham that within a year Sarai will bear a son to him and he should be called Isaac. In spite of both Abraham and Sarai being beyond normal childbearing age and Sarai being barren, he believes God.*

*God visits Abraham and again promises that he will become the father of a great nation. He makes a covenant, an agreement with Abraham assuring him that He is serious. Circumcision is the sign of the covenant and Abraham is to become circumcised and must circumcise all the male children in his household.*

*Abraham is officially renamed Abraham by God and Sarai becomes Sarah. They soon have a son Isaac, who will be his heir and who will continue God's work of building a great nation. When Isaac was a young boy, God asks Abraham to take Isaac to a far-off mountain and sacrifice him to God. As abhorrent as it is, human sacrifice was common at the time. Abraham obeys God's instructions and at the last minute*

> before this unspeakable crime is to occur, God supplies a ram for the sacrifice instead. God then acknowledges Abraham's loyalty and reliability in his willingness to sacrifice his only son.
>
> The message for me is that we need to be politely persistent in our prayer life with God, as Abraham was. Prayer does not avert evil and catastrophes in this world but unites us with God where we begin to see the events unfolding around us as God would.
>
> St. John Chrysostom (347-407 C.E.) taught that prayer is the place of refuge for every worry, a foundation for cheerfulness, a source of constant happiness, a protection against sadness."

Father in heaven, thank you for the holiday with my family and from my siblings for driving me to and from the airports.

## Monday, January 11
## Office work on my day off

> Mantra for the Day:
>
> "Give thanks to the Lord and bless his name, for the Lord is good; his steadfast love endures forever and his faithfulness to all generations" (Book of Psalms, ch. 100, v. 4-5).

Fred emailed today to say that he and Thelma would volunteer to chair the Developing Nations program. Their two boys, Chad and Chuck were mature enough to manage the farm leaving them with time to contribute to the parish and to the community. Mabel had talked to Thelma about her cross-Canada fund-raising tour and the court challenges and is concerned about her lack of time to give to this new program. Fred indicated that he and Thelma were a good team and have the time. Mabel, while she was now unable to devote the time the Developing Nations program needed, has agreed to remain involved but only peripherally and on a consulting basis.

Paul phoned to provide me with an update on the discriminatory class action suit. His colleagues in Ottawa have advised him that while constitutionally possible, to take all the dioceses of Canada to court it would take forever. In addition, each diocese is an independent entity. So, he was advised that Mabel should pick one diocese to start the class action suit. Mabel thinks that they should start with your diocese. It is her diocese too. Paul conceded that it made sense as she could provide better evidence. He apologized for any pain and stress this court case may cause, but he also thought that if anyone was capable to ride this matter out, it was me. I thanked for his vote of confidence. He advised that the Diocese should get legal representation. He recommended Peter Ziegler from his office. He is a very objective and rational adviser but unfortunately not a Catholic. On the other hand, an inexperienced Catholic lawyer could be intimidated by this court case and thereby be ineffectual. Paul also recommended Maggie too. She will spend the next six months at home and wants legal work. She will be a good asset to you, being able to see and explain both sides of the issues. You might need that information when meeting with your fellow bishops. You will be served papers next Monday and he thought a short hearing would take three days.

Father Raj emailed me to say that he and Masala were married civilly on Friday, December 31. Two members from Masala's university faculty were their witnesses. Could I bless their marriage at St. Francis? He thought that they were going to need some marital advice from one of the couples from St. Francis that attended a Priest's deanery meeting in the Fall. Could I recommend one or two of them? I replied to Father Raj's inquiry by emailing him Fred and Thelma's contact info.

I phoned Father Mike and advised him of Paul's phone call and Father Raj's email. He invited me to dinner. I agreed. Later that evening, Father Mike asked me if I was worried about this upcoming Court case? No, I replied. Surprisingly, I was not. I suggested to him that we had to meet this matter head on. Let's not put up too big a fight that we could lose and cost us more money that we do not have. I continued that in my opinion, the Holy Spirit was guiding the Church and this development. I also felt that the Courts would support the CWA's position as we move in the direction of a democratic society. There is no historical legal protection for the Church in this situation. The colonial days are long past when the reigning Government and the Church were united in developing this country and were cut a lot of slack. That alliance protected the Church from all kinds of problems but fortunately such protection does not exist today. At the end of the day, the Holy Spirit will guide us through this and it is best for us to avoid putting up any obstacles. He asked whether we, he and I were not protecting the Church enough in this situation by being so passive? I replied that I did not know. Father Mike, I asked, are we being too soft or are we cooperating with the Holy Spirit?

Turning the conversation to the subject of Father Raj, I asked him for his thoughts. Father Mike replied that they are both clearly excommunicated by the Church. I asked if we should encourage him to join the Anglican Diocese. He has already talked to Claire. After giving my question some thought, in his usual careful manner, he recommended that given all the challenging issues that we were dealing with, the Anglican Church offered him more than the Catholic Church could at this time. I emailed Father Raj with our decision that the Diocese is struggling with some major issues and would not be able to accommodate him at this time. Father Mike and I suggest that you approach Claire and the Anglican Church. I assured him that in spite of our inability to welcome him into the Catholic

Church now as a married priest, I wanted to keep connected to him. He replied thanking me.

Father in heaven, thank you for Father Mike and his sage advice. Please keep him safe and healthy to permit him to coach me through these challenging issues. Will Father Raj take us to Court for discriminatory practices given all the Anglican married priests who have joined the Church? Thank you for your love and attention. Amen

## Tuesday, January 12
## Scripture study "Job"

> Mantra for the Day:
>
> "For my thoughts are not your thoughts, nor are your ways my ways, says the Lord. For as the heavens are higher than the earth, so are my ways higher than your ways and my thoughts than your thoughts" (Book of Isaiah, ch. 55, v. 8-9).

## Summary of notes concerning my study of Job:

- The Book of Job concerns itself with the study of evil in the world. Why do bad things happen to good people?
- The story begins with Job, a very wealthy man who is lives a good and morally upright life. He has a large family and a large estate comprised of land and animals.
- God boasts about Job and his character but Satan argues that Job's good behavior is the result of all the good things that exist in his life. Satan alleges that if Job loses his family, his herds and his wealth, he too, will turn against God and curse Him. God disagrees.

- However, to prove his point, God gives Satan permission to take away Job's children, his herds and his wealth but not to take away his life.
- Soon, Job loses everything and goes into mourning but continues to bless God.
- Satan then gets God's permission to inflict Job with horrible skin sores. Job's wife encourages him to curse God and die. Job refuses but tries to understand these challenging events in his life.
- He is visited by three old friends who accompany him in his mourning. They eventually state that he must have sinned to merit such bad things in his life. The prevailing Jewish teaching at the time was that God rewarded good people with good things and punished bad people with loss and sickness. One of them even states that Job probably deserves greater punishment than he has received.
- Job scorns their wisdom but begins to question his relationship with God. Why does God judge human behavior if he can so easily forgive their bad behavior? Can humans really appease God's need for just and upright behavior? To make matters worse, God is unseen and his ways so mysterious and beyond human understanding. Is prayer ever effective? He even admits that he does not understand himself enough to plead his case before God.
- His friends are offended that he scorns their advice. They argue that his questioning is an avoidance from dealing with his own evil behavior.
- Job laments that God allows wicked people to prosper while countless other innocent people suffer. He wants to confront God but cannot find him.
- God finally responds to Job in the silence of the wind. He explained how He created the world and His power extends over all things. God asks Job where was

he when the heavens were created; when land was separated from water at the beginning of time.
- Job acknowledges that his knowledge of God is very limited and will never be able to understand God's plan for the world. God in turn, is pleased with Job's humble response but is very critical of his friends for giving him such poor advice. Job advocates for them and they are forgiven.
- God in the end, restores his wealth. Job has more children.

Takeaways:

- There are a number of stories or parables in the Gospels where the teachings are subtle and could be misconstrued. In one such parable, Jesus pays all the labourers the same daily wage regardless of how many hours they worked. The landlord in his story pays the latecomers the same wage as those who worked all day in the sun in spite of the complaints of the first to arrive for work. At the outset, this does not seem fair. However, this parable is not about social justice, but portrays a loving Father who will welcome all even latecomers into heaven. Like the story of Job, the plan of our loving Father in heaven can be challenging to understand.
- God works in mysterious ways, well beyond our comprehension. We will never be able to know or understand why God allows the things to happen He does.
- Catastrophes of one kind and another such as floods, hurricanes, and tornados should not be attributed to God as being angry with us.

At 1:00 pm, my phone rang. The Sheriff of the Court wanted to serve me with papers. He asked where could he find me to do so. I gave him the address of the Diocesan office. I would be there tomorrow, Wednesday at 10:00 am.

Ned emailed me asking if there was something he could do for me. Mabel is very busy on her cross-Canada fund-raising project and is away a lot. Could his business background be a benefit to me? I asked him when he could come to dinner and he asked if tonight was too soon. Not if you like pizza. I told him that I am now making my own pizza. Would he be OK with pepperoni, mozzarella cheese, olives and basil on his pizza? Yes.

Ed phoned wanting to know when we would be defining the job description for the Communications Director. I invited him to come for dinner if he was free. Yes, Elaine was working an afternoon shift. I informed him that Ned was also invited.

Ned arrived at 5:45 pm. He came with good news; Susan gave birth to a healthy seven-pound baby girl. Mabel had invited Susan and baby to come and live with them while she organized the next stage of her life.

At 6:00 pm Ed arrived with his two bottles of his favorite Montepulciano D'Abruzzo. Ed wanted to know my expectations. I said that we have already agreed to two days a week and let's see how that works. The Diocese needs a newspaper, journal, radio and television communications person on our staff to keep everyone informed with all these upcoming changes. Your primary obligation for the two days is to the Diocese. You can fulfill your obligations and duties to your local newspaper and to the Toronto Tribune on the other three days a week. In addition, you cannot report or discuss on any matter pertaining to this Diocese without my prior approval. Agreed? Agreed. That means that you must get my approval for any information that you send to your buddy, the Cardinal in Toronto concerning this diocese. Agreed?. Agreed. I also want you to give Father Mike and I as well as the Diocesan Pastoral Council a news briefing once a week on what is happening in the world that I may not be aware of. Agreed? Agreed. I am still prepared to pay you $100.00 an hour. Is that enough? I was assured that it was a good starting wage. I then explained to them the diocesan financial situation resulting from Father Ryan's court hearing. The finance committee was recommending selling the Cathedral. Ned, I was hoping that you could represent the diocese and try to get a good deal for us. Both Ed and Ned agreed that they were working in unfamiliar territory. I assured them that we did not want a deal that could bounce back to bite us in years to come. Ed, I hope that you will assist me in communicating with the Bishops of Canada, the parishes in this diocese, the priests, the local media outlets and the community

I emailed Charles and advised that Ned Armstrong would be my personal representative on the sale of the Cathedral and forwarded to him Ned's contact info.

Peter Ziglier emailed asking for a meeting. I suggested tomorrow at my City office at 1:00 pm. I gave him the address.

Father in heaven, thank you for your wisdom and strength to keep my wits about me. This is a very challenging time for this little Diocese in the hinterland of Western Canada. Please guide me in the days ahead. Thank you for Ed, Ned, Charles and Peter. Keep them in the warmth of your love.

## Wednesday, January 13
## Bad news/Good news

>Mantra for the Day:
>
>"The Lord is my shepherd; I shall not want. He leads me to lie down in green pastures: he leads me beside still waters. He restores my soul. He leads me in right paths for his name's sake. for you are with me; Even though I walk through the darkest valley, I fear no evil; for you are with me; your rod and your staff shall comfort me. You prepare a table before me in the presence of my enemies" (Book of Psalms, ch. 23, v. 1-5a).

At 10:00 am, I was served an envelope by the Sheriff but was afraid to open it. I had a soup and sandwich lunch with my colleagues at the Cathedral. They are such a good distraction from my stressful world. Too early to share all the problems with them.

At 1:00 pm, Peter arrived and we went through the normal get-to-know-you ritual; who we mutually knew and did not know. I suggested that we have a preliminary meeting with Paul and Mabel to find out her desired outcomes from this Court action. He explained that this type of legal work was new for everyone and exploratory in nature. I explained to him that I would prefer to settle this matter outside of Court if possible. He asked if I had read the lawsuit. I apologized saying that I was trying to avoid it. He phoned Paul who put us on hold while he phoned Mabel. It was agreed that the four of us would meet in Paul's office on Friday at 10:00 am. I asked Peter to hold off on any work on this file until after the meeting on Friday. He agreed. Then he read me the demands:

"The charges are: For long standing discriminatory practices against Canadian Catholic women, the class action suit requests the Court:

- to require this Catholic Diocese to pay in damages $25 million dollars in compensation to the Catholic Women's Association (CWA) of St. Francis Catholic Parish; or
- to require this Catholic Diocese to allow all women over thirty-five years of age and who believe to be called by the Holy Spirit, to begin training for the deaconate that would enable them to act on behalf of the Catholic Church to baptise, confirm, distribute the Eucharist, grant general absolution, dispense the sacrament of the sick, preside at weddings and funerals; and
- to require this Catholic Diocese to allow all women over thirty-five years of age and who believe to be called by the Holy Spirit, to begin a Catholic Church

- sponsored theological training program for ordination to the priesthood and upon completion and judged to be a suitable candidate, to be expeditiously ordained to the Catholic priesthood; and
- to require this Catholic Diocese to provide a validly-ordained and in good-standing Bishop of the Catholic Church to carry out these ordinations within two weeks after the candidates have completed their training and are judged to be suitable for both the diaconate and the priesthood; and
- to decree that in the event of delays from carrying out these Court mandated actions, the Court will fine this Catholic Diocese in question $50,000.00 a month in penalties and demand the closure of a parish church under the administrative control of this Catholic Diocese."

Peter looked at me gravely, stating that this class action suit was virtually airtight with little wiggle-room; a typical Paul Taylor piece of legal work. He is a very thorough lawyer. Maggie and I will start looking for weaknesses and loopholes when you give us the go ahead. We agreed that we should sit down and listen to Paul and Mabel before doing any work. Maggie is invited to the Friday meeting too if she is interested.

I emailed Archbishop Ben in Quebec City outlining the details of this class action suit. He asked me to email him the details of the suit. He said that he did not see this coming and felt bad to have left just as this was about to blow up in my face. He said that he would consult some of his Bishop colleagues and the Cardinal in Toronto and get back to me. I reminded him that we had no money for expensive lawyers and there were severe financial penalties if we used delaying tactics.

I invited Claire, her husband Cliff and two sons, John and Charles for dinner. Cliff is a science teacher at the local high school and the boys are in University. Over a dinner of roast turkey breast, roasted vegetables, mashed potatoes and mother's apple pie, we slowly got to know one another. Claire is very appreciative to be able to share St Francis Church and Cliff indicated that Claire is so much more relaxed with this arrangement. I inquired if Father Raj had approached her. She said that he has and she has forwarded his request to her Bishop. The five of us ate all of the turkey and every scrap of leftovers. Cliff was impressed with my cooking. I assured him that my mother's coaching and apple pie made a big contribution.

Father in heaven, Thank you for this very stressful and challenging day. On the one hand, I feel pressure to support Mabel's class action suit and that my parishioners are probably having mixed feelings about her case. On the other hand, I also feel pressure from the Bishops and leaders of the Canadian Catholic Church who will judge me as unfit for leadership in the Church, too soft for the heavy lifting the Bishops are expected to do, fearful of defending the traditions of the Church even though they are considered by many to be out of date and irrelevant to current societal demands. Again, I ask your guidance, please send the Holy Spirit to guide me and give me the courage required to this challenging work. I pray for the Pope, the Bishops, the priests of the diocese, my family and my parishioners. Keep them in your love. Thank you for all you do for me.

# Thursday, January 14
# Worry, stress and a CWA meeting

> Mantra for the Day:
>
> "Then Jesus said to the crowd, 'take care to guard against all greed, for though one may be rich, one's life does not consist of possessions'" (Gospel of Luke, ch. 12, v. 15).

Maggie called to find out how I was handling the worry and stress. I replied not too good. The worst part was the waiting for things to happen. She assured me that I could phone her any time and just talk about it. She reminded me that she is experiencing the same waiting experience with her pregnancy. She will remain at home until the baby is born and the family has agreed to help raise the child. They have given it a lot of thought and prayer and believe that just as Mary and Joseph were asked to raise Jesus, the Son of God, so this is an opportunity for them to do something similar with her "silent partner" who now is kicking and moving in her tummy. When I asked about her due date, she replied any day as she was in her ninth month. The family is very excited about their new family member.

She turned the subject to the Court case saying that she had asked her father for work and he has assigned her to work with Peter. She has turned down the opportunity to join us on Friday as she has grown quite large with this little infant in her tummy. I thanked her for her willingness to help and told her that I thought she would be a big asset.

At 7:30 pm, the full CWA committee met in the rectory boardroom. I opened the meeting with a prayer and then we talked at some length of the class action suit. I asked Mabel if I have explained it adequately. She smiled politely and said yes. Thelma then asked what the Diocese was going to do. I explained the repercussions if the Diocese were to win this case, every Catholic woman in the world would be angry and even more disappointed in the Church. However, if the Diocese were to lose, change in the Church would be required. Win or lose, every other diocese in Canada and even the world could be served with a similar class action suit. But, I am unable to be more specific at this time. If I was a gambling man, I would recommend that you ladies should consider what new role you would like to play in the Church; becoming either a deacon or a priest. Our lawyer, Peter Ziegler and I will be meeting with a group of Bishops next week. The ladies seem pleased. Mabel asked if she had offended me with this class action suit. I reassured her that the opposite was true. I am very appreciative for this initiative except that it has given me a ton of unexpected work. I am not able to bring about these long overdue changes to the Church by myself but members of the Church like you can. I feel very privileged to being a part of it. I thanked Mabel for taking this massive project on. Then I gave her a quick hug.

  Father in heaven, my apologies for my poor performance today. Thank you for sending the Holy Spirit to coach me through the CWA meeting. To minimize my new stresses, I watched a wild card NFL game between the Buffalo Bills and the Arizona Cardinals. Please take care of all the people that I normally pray for. Thank you.

# Friday, January 15
# Meeting of the key players in
# the Class action suit

Mantra for the Day:

"Therefore, I tell you, do not worry about your life (or your work) and what you are to eat, or about your body and what you will wear. For life is more than about food and the body more than clothing. Notice the ravens; they do not sow or reap; they have neither storehouse nor barn, yet God feeds them. How much more important are you than the birds! Can any of you by worrying add a moment to your lifespan? If even the smallest things are beyond your control, why are you anxious about the rest? (Gospel of Luke, ch. 12, v. 22-26).

At 10:00 am, I was welcomed into a small boardroom at Paul's office. Mabel, dressed to the nines as usual, was already there. I accepted a cup of strong coffee and then Paul and Peter entered the room. After the usual pleasantries, Paul wanted to know the purpose of the meeting. Peter was going to respond on our behalf but I put up my hand to signal my desire to answer. I thanked the three of them for making themselves available given their very busy work lives. I asked Peter to call this meeting to see if we could negotiate a solution thereby avoiding utilizing the Courts. Paul replied what particular items would you like to negotiate on? I responded saying that the timing is very tight and the money is beyond our ability to raise since the Father Ryan court case. He continued that they have a strong case and it has been strengthened by this information, copies of which he slid across the table to Peter and I. He encouraged us to read the information contained on it.

This sheet outlined the following points:

1. the Catholic population world-wide has doubled in size from 653 million in 1970 to 1.3 billion in 2017.
2. There are the same number of priests 415,000 in 2017 as there were in 1970.
3. 49,000 parishes have been closed due a shortage of priests.
4. This priest shortage has been under discussion in the Vatican since 1960.
5. The age of priests has increased with many ready to now retire.
6. The numbers of students studying for the priesthood are at half of the 1970 levels.
7. A solution currently utilized is to close and link parishes together contrary to the desires of many parishioners.
8. Many parishes are administered by lay people to dispense the sacraments but have not benefitted from a theological training program.
9. The use of deacons to supplement the manpower shortage has recently been reactivated but only for men, further extending this discriminatory practice.
10. The Church teaches that the Eucharist is the food for our spiritual journeys but can only be provided by a validly ordained, celibate male priest.
11. There approximately 145 women priests who are validly ordained and working in the world that are serving small communities but are not recognized by the Catholic Church.
12. Social research has concluded that a majority of Catholics will support male and female, married, single or gay priests.
13. The sex abuse scandal and the cover up have severely diminished the moral authority of the Catholic Church.
14. The Catholic Church is viewed in Canada as a public institution given that it has a government recognized charitable status, pays no property taxes and is publicly recognized as a service organization.

15. This Catholic diocese's current treatment of women is in violation of their Canadian Constitutional rights.
16. The Catholic Church appears to be "a secret private old boys club that is only accountable to the Pope in Rome and lacks transparency and accountability of its actions."

 I looked at Peter and signalled an end to this meeting. There was literally no room for negotiation on this case. Paul asked when could he file the class action suit at the Provincial Court. I thanked him but said that the Diocese would need time to consult the Bishops of Canada. He countered by asking how much time did the Diocese need. I asked for twenty-one business or working days. He replied firmly, no, only fourteen business days. He continued that the Court will look at this submission, review its merits and judge if the suit has enough legal merit to proceed. If the Court decides that there is merit in the case, the Court will appoint a judge and set aside three days for verbal submissions. A final decision could take days or weeks. I thanked Mabel and Paul for their time and we left.

 After leaving Paul's office, I asked Peter where we could find another good strong cup of coffee. He pointed out a very good coffeehouse around the corner. Having ingested a kerosene tasting espresso coffee, I asked Peter for his impressions. He apologized by saying that his lack of knowledge of the Catholic Church precluded him from giving an opinion. He volunteered that 15 business days ended on February 02. He then turned it back to me. After an uncomfortable period of silence, I confessed that his legal knowledge and experience could probably be better put to use helping me to work on the Canadian bishops. I asked him to please repackage the information contained in the class action suit and the new information provided today that we would forward to the Cardinal in Toronto and my friend, the Archbishop of Quebec. I asked him to highlight the Courts demand for broad information normally considered by the Catholic Church as private and confidential. He promised to have it ready for Monday morning.

I had lunch with Father Mike and laid out all the details. He looked alarmed and like he had just seen a ghost. I assured him that things were going to work out fine, just not as we had hoped or planned.

After lunch, I phoned Archbishop Ben with the latest details. Without waiting for his response, I asked him about the possibility that this small Diocese avoid the Court's hearing and become instead an "Ad Experimentum" project (an experiment) where the Diocese quietly tests out these ideas while keeping a very low profile. I reminded him that current Church research has confirmed that 75% of Church respondents support a married clergy, either male, female or gay. I advised him that I had hired Ed Malone thereby putting a muzzle on his hotline to the Cardinal. He hung up saying he would talk to the Cardinal. He was re-assuring and said that Father Mike and I would not be thrown under the bus.

I emailed Charles, the head of the Diocesan Finance Committee, requesting he proceed with the sale of the Cathedral. I concluded by asking him to get the best price possible. I then emailed the Archbishop and Father Mike on the pending sale of the Cathedral necessitated by the Father Ryan court case.

By 8:00 pm, during an NHL hockey game, Archbishop Ben got back to me asking to bring the young lawyer to Toronto for a Wednesday afternoon meeting. I texted Peter with the message that we needed him in Toronto for a Wednesday meeting. I phoned Margaret asking her to please arrange two tourist-class airplane tickets to Toronto either Tuesday afternoon or Wednesday morning. She replied, done. I still don't think that Margaret sleeps.

Father in heaven, thank you again for all the challenges you placed in my path today. Thank you for my helpers today including Peter, Maggie, Margaret, Ed even Mabel and Paul. I pray for the Cardinal, Archbishop Ben and all the Bishops of Canada.

# Saturday/Sunday, January 16/17
# Preach on "Praying with Job"

Mantra for the Day:

"But to you who hear I say, love your enemies, do good to those who hate you, bless those who curse you, pray for those who mistreat you. To the person who strikes you on one cheek, offer the other one as well and from the person who takes your cloak, do not withhold even your tunic" (Gospel of Luke, ch. 6, v. 27-29).

## Preach: Praying with Job

*"Dear Friends, I would like to thank you for coming to Mass this Sunday given your busy lives. My subject today is about Job. Who is Job? He is a significant Old Testament figure. He is associated with those of us who suffer for no justifying reason. According to the Old Testament, he was a wealthy man, blameless and careful to avoid doing evil. Satan, the devil, appears in front of God and alleges that Job is only a good man because he is wealthy and blessed by God. Job would not be such a good person if he was poor.*

*So, God, believing that Job is a deeply committed good person, agrees to allow the devil to test him. God takes away his wealth including his herds and property. Job struggles to understand what is happening to him but continues to praise and be appreciative to God. God tests him further. Soon, he experiences bodily sores and loneliness. His friends, relying on Old Testament wisdom, tell him that he must have sinned to have such horrible things happen to him. He argues with his friends and asserts that he is still blameless. Job requested a meeting with God to get to the bottom of this problem. Finally, God grants him a meeting in which Job wants to know what is going on. God reminds Job that just as he was not around at the beginning of time, he has a very limited understanding of what can happen. Job will never completely understand God's plan for the human race. Just as a child will not understand the difficult decisions that their parents may be required to make. After spending time with God, he was able to see things more from God's perspective. In the end, Job is satisfied with the answers he received.*

*We all know and hear about good people who are suffer from some unexplainable tragedy or a sudden unexpected illness. It disturbs us and it is difficult for us to understand and to console them. I think as we have learned from this story of Job, there probably just isn't a satisfying explanation. But if we spend time with our Father in heaven, we can better understand what is happening from His perspective. We can also just be with those who are suffering pain and loss without having to say anything."*

## Dinner with Father Mike

Sunday dinner with Sis and her family was cancelled due to a flu bug rampant in her house. So, I invited myself to Father Mike's place for dinner. It was a welcomed experience as compared to our noisy boisterous family dinners. His Sunday evenings are normally very quiet so he and I had some uninterrupted time alone. His heart pain was again under control.

I updated him on the latest developments with Paul and the feasibility of an appeal, the sale of the Cathedral as recommended by Charles and my dad and brother's suggestions. He mentioned that he spoke to a Montreal priest-colleague while I was away. His colleague explained that the Montreal Archdiocese had sold a Church that was no longer needed. A developer maintained a portion of the exterior of the building and converted it into very attractive apartments. That is such an interesting idea. Leaving his rectory, we agreed our that we needed to pray for the wisdom of Solomon.

I phoned Mabel and asked her if she would permit me to broaden the categories of future candidates for the deaconate and priesthood to include men and representatives from the LGBTQ2S+ community. She quickly agreed, asking how this would unfold. I said that it would not be part of her class action suit, but would be part of the Church's response to it. We would argue that without including these two groups, the Church would still be promoting discriminatory and sexist attitudes. She agreed and said that she would alert Paul.

Father in heaven, thank you for all your help and kindness in my work on your behalf. A special thank you for Father Mike, Mabel, Paul and the parishioners of St. Francis, St Brigid and St. Joseph.

# Monday, January 18
# Day off and Men's Club meeting

Mantra of the Day:

"Beloved, let us love one another, because love is of God; everyone who loves is born of God and knows God" (First Letter of John, ch. 4, v. 7).

Peter phoned asking me if I wanted to review his report before he emailed to the Archbishop Ben and to the Cardinal's office in Toronto. I said, No. But the sooner they get it the better. I asked him to please send me a copy for my records.

Charles emailed to say that the Cathedral has been advertised for sale privately for two weeks. They have one offer and he and Ned have been negotiating with the purchaser. There are two parts to it; a) they will pay 1.5 million or b) 1.2 million if the Diocese would like the title to a 1400 square foot, 2-bedroom, 2-bathroom apartment once the construction is complete. The Diocese would be responsible for taxes, condo fees and utilities of the apartment. The Diocese would also lease 1200 square feet for a small chapel at $1.40 per square foot a month. The Diocese would be responsible for utilities and cleaning. We have 48 hours to respond.

At 7:30 pm, the men's club began with a small prayer. Ed Malone joined our usual cohort of men from the parish and was warmly received. The meeting focused on the class action suit. After hearing all the details, Bill asked about the future of married priests. If women in the Church become the favored sex, men and women will just have switched roles; nothing really will have changed. Colin wanted to know where the members of the men's club could study theology in anticipation of eventually being ordained. A lively discussion followed with a lot of questions, many opinions and few answers.

Before Ed left the rectory, I asked him to prepare a draft of a Diocesan newsletter to be mailed to every parish in the diocese. It should focus on the departure of Bishop Ben, that Father Mike and I would be managing the diocese until the Vatican had selected a replacement and the Father Ryan court case with the results and the large financial compensation required. He said that he needed a day to prepare it and would send you as copy for your review.

My last work task of the day was to read Peter's report. It seemed to be extremely well done, very professional and very legalese.

Father in heaven thank you for Peter, Ed and the Men's Club. Please keep the men in your protection. Thank you for your wisdom and guidance today.

## Tuesday, January 19
## Scripture study "Moses" and
## Preparing for Toronto

Mantra for the Day:

"God passed before him (Moses) and proclaimed, (I am) 'God, a God of mercy and grace, endlessly patient - so much love, loyal in love for a thousand generations, forgiving iniquity, rebellion and sin. Still, He doesn't ignore sin. He holds sons and daughters responsible for a father's sins to the third and fourth generations'" (Book of Exodus, ch. 34, v. 6-7).

# Scripture Study: Summary notes of Moses
# Moses (1390 – 1270 BCE)

1. Moses is considered the most important Old Testament prophet. He is incorrectly credited as the author of the first five books of Old Testament, known as the Torah.
2. Four hundred years have passed since Joseph had welcomed his family into Egypt. There was now a new Pharaoh in charge who did not know Joseph or what he had accomplished for the Pharaoh. This new Pharaoh observed that the population of Israelites (Hebrews) was growing faster than the Egyptian population and was worried.
3. He ordered repressive measures to make their lives more difficult, such as demanding that they had to find their own straw for the brick making while maintaining the same levels of production. He also ordered the Hebrew midwives to kill the male Hebrew babies. The midwives fearing their God refused, reporting to the Pharaoh that the Hebrew women were strong and were able to give birth without the assistance of a midwife. The Pharaoh then ordered that all Hebrew males were to be drowned in the Nile River.
4. When Moses was born, his mother was able to hid him for three months. But realizing that she could not hid him any longer, she placed him in a waterproof basket among the reeds of the Nile River. His older sister watched over him from a distance. When the daughter of the Pharaoh came to bath in the Nile, she heard the cry of an infant. She discovered it was a Hebrew boy. His sister asked the Pharaoh's daughter if she could find a Hebrew nurse for the baby. She went and got her mother to nurse the boy. Eventually, the mother gave her son to the daughter of the Pharaoh as her son.

5. When an adult, Moses observed an Egyptian beating a Hebrew male. He became incensed and impulsively killed the Egyptian and buried him in the sand. Fearing for his life, he fled to Median, where he married and had two sons.
6. One day while tending his flocks, God appeared to him in a burning bush. Moses was intrigued as the fire was not consuming the bush. As he approached the bush, God spoke to him, explaining that He has heard the cries of the enslaved Hebrews. He wants to rescue them and lead them back to Canaan, the promised land.
7. After considerable resistance, Moses eventually agreed and with his brother Aaron, approached the Pharaoh explaining that the God of the Hebrews wanted them to go on a three-day journey into the wilderness to pray. The Pharaoh initially resists and eventually the ten plagues initiated by God forced the Pharaoh's hand. The tenth plague, the Passover, has become an annual ritual among the Jewish people acknowledging God's intervention on their behalf..
8. While they were camped by the Red Sea, the Pharaoh changed his mind and mobilized his troops to recapture the escaping Hebrews. Moses raised his hand and his staff opening a dry channel for the Hebrews to escape. When the Pharaoh and his army tried to follow, the waters returned and they were destroyed.
9. Desert living was not fun. God dealt with the complaint of the Hebrews by providing quail meat at night, bread in the morning and water. God guided them with a cloud of smoke by day and pillar of fire at night. Yet the Hebrews continued to complain, stating that they would have preferred to die in Egypt.
10. At Mount Sinai, God revealed himself to Moses and Aaron as a God who liberated the Hebrews from the

Pharaoh's control. He introduced them to the concept of holiness and invited them into a covenant relationship where they would be his treasured possession of all the people. They agreed and were given the ten commandments.

11. During an extended absence of Moses, the Hebrews feeling abandoned, used their jewelry to fashion a calf to worship. This partying angered God who then threatened to destroy them. God's wrath was calmed by Moses. The covenant was renewed and God described himself as merciful, gracious, slow to anger, constant in love and faithfulness.
12. Eventually the Hebrews get back to Canaan. They now become known as Israelites.

Takeaways:

a) Our God listens to us and hears our cries for help just as He did with the Hebrews. He reaches out to us.
b) Moses developed a shining face from his frequent and lengthy meetings with God. His face was so shiny that the Hebrews could not look at him. So eventually, he covered his face when he was with them.
c) The desert provided an opportunity for the Hebrews to develop a closer relationship with God. As food, water and security were provided by God, it allowed the Hebrews to be less distracted by the demands of daily living.
d) A desert or minimalist lie-style can add a valuable perspective on our lives too.
e) As in the New Testament, John the Baptist spent his early years in the desert, surviving on locusts and honey as he prepared himself for his mission as a precursor or a messenger of Jesus.

f) Jesus begins his public life spending 40 days in the desert.

## Wednesday, January 18
## Meeting the Cardinal and the Bishops in Toronto

Mantra for the Day:

"Set a guard over my mouth, O Lord; keep watch over the door of my lips. But as my eyes are always turned towards you seeking your refuge; do not leave me defenceless" (Book of Psalms, ch. 141, v. 3-4).

After a 5:30 am alarm call (unusual for me) and dropping off my car at my parent's home, I took a taxi to the airport. Peter had already arrived.

Waiting for our flight, I sent an email to Susan Green, a colleague of Wendy's asking if she were available on February 20/21 weekend. I am organizing a married-couples retreat for our parish and wondered if she could come, talk and give advice to these mature married couples. If she was available and open to such a request, I would email her our schedule.

Our flight arrived in Toronto at 11:30 am, we had a short lunch at the airport and took a taxi to the Cardinal's office. Present were the Cardinal, Archbishop Ben and four Bishops whom neither Peter nor me knew. The Cardinal stood out, dressed in red, tall, white hair, well over six feet, appeared to be in his sixties. The four bishops looked older, were serious-looking and dressed in black with red piping, no CFL shirts in this crowd. Archbishop Ben warmly welcomed us. After introductions and coffee, we turned to the business at hand.

Peter presented the class action suit with all its gritty details. As planned, he highlighted the Court's right to subpoena

Church records that it felt it needed to adjudicate this case. He also highlighted the current poor financial status of the Diocese resulting from the Father Ryan matter and potential court costs from delays in carrying out the mandate of the Court. While not totally unexpected, the discussion focused on the Church's concern for privacy and avoiding having to reveal its business in court. The separation of Church and State protected this right. One of Bishops joked that unlike the Toronto Archdiocese, their dioceses were property rich but cash poor too. They all regretted that they were not able to offer our Diocese any financial aid.

Then Archbishop Ben introduced the concept of an "Ad Experimentum" project as a compromise solution. He reminded them of the worker-priest experiment that was tried in France and Italy in the 1950's but was unfortunately disbanded when the priests joined the unions to push for better working conditions for workers. Unions were associated with the rise of socialism and communism and thereby were judged by Pope Pius XII as too Marxist.

This project would allow women to become deacons and ultimately priests after the appropriate training and screening but only on a trial basis. The success of this experiment would be conditional on it keeping a very low profile and out of the press. I assured them that the Diocese had hired the biggest threat to the Diocese's privacy, namely the Cardinal's friend Ed Malone, who is now under contract to a local community newspaper and the Toronto Tribune. Everyone had a good laugh at the Cardinal's expense. He wanted more details. Ed is under contract to our diocese 2 days a week and must get prior approval from the Diocese to publish any Diocesan news either in his local newspaper or the Tribune. The Cardinal inquired how much we had agreed to pay him. I said $100.00 an hour for a maximum of two days or 16 hours a week. The Cardinal said that he would subsidize that salary by an additional $50.00 an hour to further ensure the privacy of the Diocese.

The meeting continued discussing the pros and cons of this proposed "experiment". The Cardinal inquired who the lawyer was for the women. I replied it was Paul Taylor, a good Catholic middle-aged westerner who comes highly recommended even by his colleagues. The Cardinal muttered that he needed someone of his ability working for him.

The meeting ended at 5:00 pm and the Cardinal took me aside and inquired about the Benedictine project for the protective custody of convicted pedophiles. I advised him that I did not have an up-to-date answer for him but would check with Father Joe upon my return and email him with an update. He gave us their assurance that they would get back to us in a few days on whether we could proceed with this deaconate training program for women. Archbishop Ben joined us for dinner in our hotel before returning to the Cardinal's home for the night. Peter and I ended our day by watching a Toronto-Montreal hockey game on TV.

I asked Peter if he was a betting person, what outcome would he bet on?

He replied Paul Taylor and the experiment.

I agreed.

Charles emailed that option A, the 1.5 million was a simple, legally clean sale and what he would recommend. Fred (and of course Thelma) and Ned both recommended option B as the value of the apartment and the chapel would increase in time being a part of a new building. They also suggested that we ask them to give the Diocese the land title for the Chapel space too. I responded to Charles and Ned to pursue option B with the inclusion of the title for the Chapel.

Father in heaven, thank you for making all these arrangements today. Thank you for the Pope, the Vatican officials, the Cardinal, the Bishops, for Paul, Mabel and Peter who are challenging me on how to love broadly and unconditionally. Thank you for Charles, Ned and Fred.

# Thursday, January 21
# Return flight

Mantra for the Day:

"Lord, help me to live this day, quietly, easily and to lean upon your great strength. Assist me to wait for the unfolding of your will, patiently and serenely. Assist me to meet others, peacefully, joyously and to face today and tomorrow, confidently and courageously." (St. Francis of Assisi 1183 -1226).

Our morning flight home was great. A big load off my mind. The ball was now in the Bishops' court. I advised Peter that we now had to just wait. I also informed him that I would be including mature men and gays and trans gender (men and women) in the list of potential candidates. To exclude them would result in another court battle. I will inform the Cardinal, Archbishop Ben and the other Bishops.

With the time change, I was able to have lunch with Father Mike. I explained in great detail who was at this meeting, what was said and what the focus was. He was not surprised that the privacy and the secrecy of the Church had become their priority. He congratulated me again and repeated that he felt that the Diocese was in good hands under my leadership. To my inquiry about the state of his health, he said that he is starting to think of winding down.

I answered the DeMarco's longstanding invitation for dinner. I am getting to dislike eating alone. They were very pleasant but full of questions on what the Parish and the Town is going to look like with the proposed changes. Mario is an ambitious businessman. I assured them that the Town and the Parish will work together in addressing change and while this change may feel uncomfortable, it will be for the best for everyone. Isabella served Basa fish, linguini pasta, steamed carrots and broccoli along with a Caesar salad. Scrumptious. Their two teenage children Mark and Stella were positively delightful, energetic and fun.

At 10:00 pm after procrastinating all day, I emailed the Cardinal, Bishop Ben and the four Bishops that I was taking the liberty of including mature men and mature gays and transgender both men and women, as eligible candidates for the diaconate program. To do anything less would trigger another court process. Only Bishop Ben acknowledged my email.

Father in heaven, thank you again for another successful day. Thank you for the Bishops, Peter and the DeMarco family. Father, you treat me royally. How can I ever thank you?

## Friday, January 22
## Waiting for a decision and sale of the Cathedral

Mantra for the Day:

"O Holy Spirit, descend plentifully into my heart. Enlighten the dark corners of my mind and body."
(St. Augustine 354 – 430 CE)

9:00 am Archbishop Ben emailed me stating the committee of Bishops have decided to take our situation to the Pope and the Vatican in Rome. They have a meeting with the Pope on Monday afternoon scheduled for 5:00 pm Rome time. They are prepared to support your solution of having the Diocese become an "Ad Experimentum" project on the following conditions: 1) that this experiment is kept out of the press until the Pope and the Vatican agree to publicize it, 2) the class action suit cannot go a public trial, 3) all the documents from both sides become the property of the Vatican, 4) the Pope and the Vatican also need to approve this special Church project. I emailed him back saying that the deadline for their support was February 02. Without that agreement, Paul Taylor would file the papers with the Court. He acknowledged the deadline. I emailed their four conditions to Paul.

I immediately phoned Father Mike with the good news. He was relieved and congratulated me. The secrets of the Catholic Church and the Vatican were still safe. I assured him that there were probably other problems soon to surface so we should enjoy the good times while they last.

I also phoned Peter but was only able to leave a long congratulatory message on his voicemail. I also asked him to contact Paul who hopefully would pass on this message to Mabel. I emailed Mabel and suggested she talk to Paul.

Charles and Ned emailed to say that the purchase was finalized with option B with the inclusion of the title for the Chapel. They stipulated that the Chapel be interdenominational and open to everyone for quiet meditation. I agreed.

Ed emailed me a draft of the first diocesan newsletter.

I had dinner with Fred, Thelma, Chad and Chuck that was very pleasant. The subject of religion did not come up once, thank goodness. Fred and Thelma chatted with some excitement about the Developing Nations program. He had talked with Archbishop Ben who would join them on a trip to Ecuador, Peru and Haiti. It was the Archbishop's opinion that these three countries would be more receptive to North American assistance with housing, clean water facilities and soccer fields. They would travel for two weeks beginning in mid-February. When I asked them about where they would get their money for this program, Thelma jumped in saying that they are working on expanding their casino from two days to four days and she and Fred were going to take the lead on starting the lottery. Their goal is to raise a million dollars a year for both the Diocese and the Developing Nations project. They are also exploring the idea of channeling all their fundraising profits into a charitable foundation. Foundations have special tax benefits. They took my breath away.

Father in heaven, thank you for the good news from the Bishops. Thank you too for Fred and Thelma. Keep then all in your embrace. As usual, I pray for the Pope and those working in the Vatican, the Canadian Bishops and ask that you inspire them as you inspire me.

## Saturday/Sunday, January 23/24
## Preach "Moses"

Mantra for the Day:

"The Lord passed before him and proclaimed, "I am the Lord, a God merciful and gracious, slow to anger, and abounding in steadfast love and faithfulness, keeping steadfast love for the thousandth generation, forgiving iniquity and transgression and sin. Still, He doesn't ignore sin. He holds sons and grandsons responsible for a father's sins to the third and fourth generation" (Book of Exodus, ch. 34, v. 6-7).

## Preaching on "Moses"

*"My dear friends, thank you again for coming to Mass today and inviting God our loving Father into your lives today. I would like to talk about Moses. He is a very important Old Testament figure. It is estimated that he lived from 1390 to 1270 before the Common Era. The Passover, one of the many events associated with Moses is still practiced every year by many Jewish people.*

*The back story to Moses is that the Jewish people or the Israelites or the Hebrews as they were then known were living in Egypt. They had migrated there at the invitation of Joseph, the son of Jacob to avoid a famine in Canaan. Some four hundred years later, the Pharaoh saw that the Hebrew people were becoming more numerous than the Egyptians and began to oppress them. For example, the Pharaoh ordered the Hebrews to find their own straw to make the bricks they needed yet maintain same level of production as before. When this strategy did not work, he ordered all Hebrew male infants be murdered. Now Moses' mother kept his birth secret for some months and then decided to give him away. She placed him in a waterproofed basket along the Nile River where the Pharaoh's daughter bathed but under the watchful eye of Moses' little sister. When Pharaoh's daughter heard the baby cry, she was moved with pity. When the little sister approached asking if she could find a wet nurse, the daughter agreed. So, Moses was miraculously raised in his family until he was old enough to be adopted by the daughter of the Pharaoh.*

*As an adult, Moses saw an Egyptian man beating up a Hebrew man. Moses attacked him, killed him and buried him in the desert. Fleeing for his life, he became a shepherd.*

*One day he noticed a nearby bush was burning but was not consumed. Coming closer, he heard God speak to him. God explained that He was the God of his forefathers, namely Abraham, Isaac, Jacob and Joseph. He has heard the cry of His people in Egypt and wanted to help* them. He asked Moses approach the Pharaoh requesting that he allow the Hebrews to leave. Moses resisted arguing he was not suited for such a task; he was slow in speech and was not an eloquent speaker. God persisted explaining He would use his powers to assist him. To prove this point, God turned Moses staff into a snake and then back to a staff and then changed to skin on his hand to a leprous skin and then back. God was determined and threatened ten plagues, the last being the death of all first-born children and animals. God explained that he would use these events to demonstrate there was no other God than the God of Hebrews.

Yahweh began to carry out the first few plagues but still the Pharaoh persisted in defiance. The Passover detailed the ritual for the tenth plague. The Hebrews were told to share a lamb dish with herbs and be ready to leave Egypt. The blood of the lamb was to be placed on the doorposts of their homes so that the angel of death would past over it, thus the name Passover. The outcome was that the Pharaoh reluctantly allowed the Hebrews to leave. The Passover has become an annual feast where a senior person of the household tells the story of how God renewed his promise of protection to Abraham by using His power to lead the Hebrew people out of slavery in Egypt.

There is so much more to the story of Moses that will be continued on another occasion. For today, this story is a reminder that God wants to use us to carry out His plan for the human race like He did with Moses. We should pray for the strength and the courage to assist God."

## Sunday dinner with Colin, Marion and their three girls

They welcomed me warmly into their home on a typical cold Canadian winter evening. The girls, fourteen, eleven and seven years of age seemed comfortable to fit right into our conversations. Abby, the seven-year-old is the comedian in the family and had us continually giggling at her humorous comments and teasing. I learned that the three of them are both dedicated students and serious athletes. They live and breathe soccer.

The subject eventually turned to Mabel's class action suit. After Colin and Marion explained what it was about to the girls, I said that a lawyer and I had presented an alternative proposal to a group of Canadian bishops who are working on it. They have until February 02 to come up with their response. I was dreading that one of these four women would ask why women did not have the same rights as men in the Church, but thankfully they were probably coached by their parents not to ask. After two hours of a delicious chicken dinner, discussion about soccer and goofing around with Abby, I thanked them for their kind hospitality and returned to a New York-Boston NHL hockey game on TV.

Father in heaven, thank you for another day working with and for You. Thank you for Colin, Marion and the three girls and their kindness to me over dinner. Thank you for the parishioners in St. Francis, St Brigid and St. Joseph. Keep them all in your warm embrace and your love.

# Monday, January 25
# Meetings on my day off

Mantra for the Day:

"Take care not to perform your good deeds in order that people may see them and praise you; otherwise you will have no reward from your heavenly father. When you do something for someone else, do not think about how it looks. Just do it quietly. That is the way your Father in heaven, who conceived you in love, working behind the scenes, helps you out" (Book of Matthew, ch. 6, v. 1-4).

9:00 AM: I finally met with Margaret and Max today for a long meeting concerning her future status with the Diocese. Max is still as cuddly and affectionate as ever. She assured me that while it was time for her to retire, she was not going to abandon me. I asked her how much time would she give me to find a replacement for her? She replied, would by the end of the month of February work? We agreed. In the meantime, Ed would put a notice in the local newspaper that the Diocese was searching for an office manager. She also informed me that Max was part of her retirement package. I agreed.

I met with Father Joe and his colleagues Fathers Martin and Basil to inquire about the status of construction of the secure cells at the Monastery. He informed me the final plans for stage 1, were proceeding. There will twelve 12 by 12-foot apartments, not cells, complete with wooden beds and simple mattresses (Neither a Holiday Inn nor a monastery mattress) sinks, toilets, desks, bookcases, TVs and desk lamps. They expected the construction to be completed by the end of February. They have hired some local men who would undergo training to be the guards, who would be paid directly by the Federal Government. I was impressed.

He then inquired about the Diocesan Plan and I apologized and said that it was still under wraps for another couple of weeks. They love their new digs and have reported to the Abbot their activities since arriving. I then promised that as soon as the plan was approved, I would like to visit the Abbot and update him. He agreed.

I phoned the Cardinal and luckily caught him on my first call. I reported what Father Joe had informed me about the progress on the construction of a special penitentiary. He was impressed. He stated that Bishop Ben had informed him that this project at the monastery with the Benedictines was your idea. He congratulated me, thanked me for the call and quickly hung up.

Father in heaven, thank you for your inspiration and guidance today. Thank you for the Cardinal, the Abbot, Fathers Joe, Martin and Basil. A special thank you for Margaret who makes my work so easy and all those who make my life such a joy. Remember my long list of those in need of your love and forgiveness.

## Tuesday, January 26
## Scripture Study: Micah, the prophet and Parish Council meeting

Mantra for the Day:

"Beloved, let us love one another, because love is from God; everyone who loves utilizes the love that God has given them and knows God" (First Letter of John, ch. 4, v. 7).

# Micah the prophet

## Summary of notes:

Background:

1. Micah was one of four great eight-century Old Testament prophets. The four were Amos, Isaiah, Hosea and Micah.
2. His name means "Who is like Yahweh (God).
3. He grew up in a small rural community near Jerusalem.
4. He prophesized in both the Kingdoms of Israel and Judah between the years of 742 and 686 Before the Common Era (BCE).
5. Between 732 and 722 BCE, Assyrian armies conquered Damascus, parts of Israel and Samaria, Israel's capital city. At this time, Judah and Jerusalem under King Ahaz, became a new state in the Assyrian Empire.
6. Judah was experiencing a radical economic growth everywhere while living under the threat of a foreign military invasion. Business growth and development was evident. There were investments in land resulting in new large landholdings and the collapse of smaller ones. The wealthy thrived at the expense of small peasant farmers. This was accompanied by a shift from a barter economy to a mercantile economy favoring large businesses. This further increased the gap between the rich and the poor.
7. Many priests and prophets were swept up in the business side of life and stopped teaching Yahweh's message.
8. In 701 BCE, Sennacherib, King of Assyria attacked Judah causing the fall of many fortified towns but was unable to conquer Jerusalem. It was left intact, but Judah, the Kingdom, was a dominated country.

## The message of Micah:

1. He exposed social injustice and inequality.
2. He preached against the political and religious leaders because they had abandoned their divinely ordained responsibility to maintain justice throughout the land.
3. He described rites of worship as hypocritical when the plights of the poor were ignored.
4. Micah was appalled by the rich citizenry of Jerusalem who seized the properties of the poor in lieu of debt payments.
5. Homeless people especially single women with children increased as the rich acquired the lands of the poor.
6. Family life broke down as parents could not look after their children.
7. Farmers were not able to get a fair price for their produce.
8. Micah preached a return to the Mosaic Covenant made with their ancestors at Mount Sinai. Yahweh had brought the Israelites out of slavery in Egypt, taught them social justice and to care for the disadvantaged. The Covenant was not an empty ritual.
9. Micah foresaw the Assyrian invasion and predicted the desolation it would cause. Yahweh would use the coming invasion and occupation as an opportunity to ride Judah of evil.
10. But hope, not doom, was Micah's primary message. He preached a new social order and a return to Yahweh, who is merciful, whose compassion outweighs justice and whose love for all is forgiving and tolerant.

I received an email from Sis that the parents would be arriving home on Saturday afternoon.

## Parish Council meeting

At 7:00 pm, the Parish Council met in the rectory boardroom. All members were present. After a short prayer, I announced the parish married couples' weekend was now scheduled for late February. More details are to follow. Fred asked for an update on the class action suit. I smiled at Mabel and then outlined all the events that have occurred; including our trip to Toronto and the trip to Rome by a special committee of Bishops. I stated that Peter and I had proposed the diocese avoid the Court hearing and with Rome's permission, become special project where mature women over thirty-five years of age could study for both the deaconate and the priesthood and if proved suitable, would be ordained by a Bishop and approved for work in this Diocese. While it might be jumping the gun, those of you so inclined, may want to think about making an application with Margaret at our Diocesan office. Fred, to no one's surprise, had a follow up question inquiring if I thought this was fair to the men in the diocese. I replied that it was not fair to either men or the LGBTQ2S+ or the trans gender community either. So, I have emailed the Cardinal, Bishop Ben and the other Bishops that I have included mature men and male and female members of the gay and transgender community as well. So, it is time to quietly inform those mature individuals who might be good candidates. There is a requirement of secrecy about this project. The Vatican wants to keep this project a secret. The meeting ended on a very hopeful note.

Father in heaven, will I ever get things straight for everyone in this parish and the diocese? Please help me ride out this storm. Today, You revealed your desire for justice and fairness. I needed to add the men and members of LGBTQ2S+ and transgender community to the list of potential candidates. Thank you for the Freds, the Mabels and the other members of the Parish Council.

# Wednesday, January 27
# Meeting with my Interdenominational Colleagues

Mantra for the Day:

"So, I tell you: whatever you ask for in prayer, believe that you have received it, and it shall be given to you, says the Lord" (Gospel of Mark, ch. 11, v. 24).

Simone called to say that Maggie had just given birth to a seven-pound baby girl. It was an easy birth given all the sit-ups and squats that Maggie had done in the last four months. Everyone is delighted about another girl in the family especially Paul.

3:00 pm, my Interdenominational Committee colleagues entered my rectory boardroom again. They were excited to see one another after a two-month absence. The usual group was in attendance. Another detailed question and answer period on the class action law suit followed. Mabel had obviously discussed her project far and wide. What was my reaction? I replied that if this legal action resulted in the Catholic Church becoming less sexist and more inclusive, it is all to the good. Joan asked if women could become deacons and priests, what about men? Joan, I replied, that mature men and mature gays and transgenders (both men and women) have been included. Having the floor, she asked what could our group do for the community? Someone suggested a botanical garden, another suggested that we could promote a house painting program where the town office would encourage painting all the buildings in the town to give it a fresh look. The volume purchase of the paint could result in a large savings and would build a strong community experience. Excellent ideas. I suggested a girl's baseball team that could compete with the surrounding communities. We agreed to flesh out these ideas before our next meeting in late February.

Claire approached me after the meeting to say that Father Raj had applied to join the Anglican Church and his application was still under review. She asked if I would give him a good reference. I replied that I would give him an excellent reference both as a friend and as a colleague. Claire also mentioned that she had met Masala and described her as "a lovely olive-skinned beauty."

Father in heaven, thank you for the love you bestow on my parishioners, my Protestant colleagues, our community residents and those in the Diocese. A special thank you for the Taylors, Maggie and their new baby girl. Help me to avoid feeling jealous of Father Raj, Claire and Joan, ministers serving You that have partners. Keep Raj and Masala in your warm embrace. Amen

## Thursday, January 28
## Waiting is not my strong suit

Mantra for the Day:

"Blessed be the name of the Lord. From the rising of the sun to its setting, the Lord is to be praised. The Lord raises the poor from the dust and lifts the needy from the ash heap, to make them sit with princes, with the princes of his people" (Book of Psalms, ch. 113, v. 7-8).

I emailed Fred and Thelma asking if their two adult sons would run a child-care service for the married couples' weekend. We would pay them.

Today was a real day off, for a change. I did some laundry, tidied my desk at St. Francis, had lunch with Margaret, dropped off flowers for Maggie and had pizza with Ed and Elaine.

Father in heaven, still no word from Rome. Please send the Pope, the Vatican officials and the Canadian Bishops your love, inspiration and guidance. Thank you for the quiet day with no problems but the comfort of time with You and with Ed and Elaine.

## Friday, January 29
## Finally, a reply from Rome

Mantra for the Day:

"As a father has compassion for his children, so the Lord has compassion for those who love him. For he knows how we were made, he remembers that we are dust" (Book of Psalms, ch. 100, v. 13-14).

Bishop Ben emailed me to say that the Pope and the Vatican were going to support the "Ad Experimentum" project based on the terms outlined at the Toronto meeting plus two new conditions. The first new condition requires the Diocese to report monthly starting in March to the Cardinal on the progress of the program and reaffirming the security of the project. He will forward the report to the Pope and Vatican officials. Eventually that requirement could be revised to reporting bi-monthly, depending on how the Vatican evaluates the progress of this initiative. Second, the Vatican wants all correspondence on this project be written under the code name of "Diocese of Carthage". He would be emailing these conditions to me shortly. He asked if I thought that Paul and Mabel would accept the revised terms. I will know the answer your question after I meet with them soon.

I reminded the Archbishop that I had extended the invitation for the deaconate program to the men in the diocese and to the gay and transgender community. If I did not include these two groups, they would be hiring Paul Taylor. He agreed and hung up. I immediately phoned Peter and gave him the news and asked him to set up a meeting with Paul and Mabel as soon as possible. He emailed me at the end of the day to say that we have a meeting scheduled for Tuesday, February 02 at 5:00 pm.

I phoned Father Joe to inquire if he and his two colleagues could meet with me at 10:00 am Monday morning at the Cathedral boardroom to discuss some preliminary elements of the diocesan plan. He agreed. I emailed Ed asking him to sit in on this meeting. He agreed.

Simone called inviting me to dinner on Sunday. Maggie would like to introduce me to her daughter, no name yet. I apologized for being already committed to a family dinner for the first time in a month. We agreed on a Monday dinner.

Father in heaven, thank you for the good news from Rome. Everything seems to be going my way. I will sleep better tonight. As usual, please continue to love my family, my friends and my parishioners. Thank you. Time for an NHL game: Calgary Flames verses the Winnipeg Jets in Winnipeg.

## Saturday/Sunday, January 30/31
## Preach "Micah, the prophet"

Mantra for the Day:

"God (Yahweh) has made it plain how to live: Do what is fair and just to your neighbour, be compassionate and loyal in your love, and don't take yourself too seriously; but take God (Yahweh) seriously" (Book of Micah, ch. 6, v. 8).

## Preach: Micah the prophet.

"Dear friends, thank you for coming to Mass today. My topic today is Micah the prophet. He was one of four great eighth-century, old testament prophets along with Amos, Isaiah and Hosea. His name means "Who is like Yahweh (God)?" He grew up a rural community near Jerusalem. Micah preached during a time when Judah was experiencing radical internal change and living under the threat of a foreign military invasion. Judah experienced an economic revolution. Many priests and prophets were swept up in the business side of life and stopped teaching Yahweh's message. King Hezekiah, the son of Ahaz and the thirteenth king of Judah undertook many religious reforms such as allowing only the worship of Yahweh and prohibiting the veneration of false deities in the Temple in Jerusalem

Micah's message was to expose social injustice and inequity and offer hope to the people of Judah. Deeply concerned with ethical issues, he preached against the political and religious leaders as they had abandoned their divinely ordained responsibility of maintaining justice throughout the land. There were hypocritical elaborate rites of worship without concern for one's neighbours. Micah was appalled by the evil in Jerusalem where the rich are seizing the properties of the poor in lieu of debt payments. The number of homeless people especially single women with children increased as the rich confiscated the land and holdings of the poor. Farmers could not get a fair price for their *produce. Family life broke down; parents could not look after their children.*

*Micah reminded Judahites of the covenant made between Yahweh and Moses and how Yahweh brought them out of the land of Egypt and taught them social justice and to care for the disadvantaged. The covenant was not an empty ritual. Micah foresaw the Assyrian invasion and predicted the desolation it would cause; Yahweh would use this coming occupation as a wakeup call and to rid Judah of evil. But hope, not doom, was Micah's overall message. He preached a new social order and a confidence in God who is merciful, whose compassion outweighs justice and whose love for all is forgiving and tolerant.*

*When we hear the story of Micah, what is God our loving Father telling us about himself/herself? The face of God is mercy, forgiveness, justice, unconditional love. We meet God our loving Father in our spouse, in our children, in our neighbours and in our fellow citizens. In closing, Yahweh's message has made it plain on how to live: "Do what is fair and just to your neighbour, be compassionate and loyal in your love, and don't take yourself too seriously; but take God (Yahweh) seriously"*

*What would Micah preach about if he were living today? What would he be saying regarding our treatment of our homeless, our refugees, our indigenous brothers and sisters, those dying from the opioid crises and the sexual abuse victims in both the Catholic Church and in our society?"*

## Sunday dinner with family

It is amazing how fast my nieces and nephews are growing up. The boys are interested in hockey and the girls in ballet. After hearing the four of them talk about their friends and activities at school, I was invited to watch a hockey game, so the guys retreated to the family room to watch the Montreal Canadiens defeat the Toronto Maple Leafs 4-0.

Father in heaven, thank you for safeguarding my family during their vacations. My father and mother look so well rested. I have missed mother's Sunday evening dinners.

CHAPTER
4

# *Journal Entries for February*

## Monday, February 01
## Meeting with the Benedictines

Mantra for the Day:

"The saints were not superhuman. They were people who loved God in their hearts and who shared this joy with others" (Pope Francis in office since 2013).

Ed and I rode in together to the meeting at the Cathedral. He seemed hyped with enthusiasm. He informed me that the editor of the Tribune had phoned him offering him a new position at the newspaper. It was the role of manager of the civic affairs section of the Tribune and would be a substantial increase in his former salary. He wanted to know if Elaine would consider coming back to Toronto? I thanked him for the kind offer but I needed to talk to her and to my current employer.

The three Benedictines, Fathers Joe, Martin and Basil were waiting. I introduced Ed Malone as the Diocese's new communications director and explained how the Fathers Joe and his brother monks rescued me from alcoholism. After we had our second cup of coffee, I told them about the Class Action suit in some detail and the Vatican's support for our experimental project. I told Ed that his friend the Cardinal was also key to this crisis.

The result is that the Diocese can now set up a teaching program for the deaconate and one for the priesthood. Potential candidates must demonstrate their maturity and capability with good academic records, positive work evaluations and clean criminal checks. The deaconate would prepare the candidates to preach, to baptize, to confirm, to distribute the Eucharist at Mass and give the Sacrament to the Sick. Deacons, male, female or gay and trans gender persons, could then apply to study for the priesthood. The details of that program are still being worked out.

Each parish should ideally have a minimum of four deacons that can rotate to avoid having this role becoming burdensome. The program would essentially be a correspondence program with one Saturday a month for in-person learning. It should be scripture based and I would be happy to provide all my notes and handouts from my course.

So, will you my Benedictine friends put this program into action? I foresee that the deaconate would be a three to four-month program with an ordination of approved candidates by the end of June. Regarding future single or married men or women candidates for the priesthood, they should be deacons first who then feel called to a different level of commitment and service.

While the Vatican has only approved this initiative for women, I have unilaterally included mature men, married or single and mature members of the LGBTQ2S+ and trans gender community and have so advised the Cardinal, Archbishop Ben and the other Bishops. We are also doing some community service projects in the St. Francis parish. As an example, Fred and Thelma, members of St. Francis, will be developing and implementing what we are calling a Developing Nations Program. It will promote the development of housing, clean water and soccer fields in selected dioceses in South America. I can predict that eventually other dioceses will be searching for developers of such a program.

In addition to this work, I would like you to preach a four-day retreat for diocesan priests on Benedictine spirituality. This retreat format could turn into a retreat for the laity of the diocese too. The Benedictines were silent, trying to collect themselves and looking at one another. Then Father Joe said that they are feeling a little overwhelmed by what they heard today. They need some time to absorb what they heard and discuss it with the Abbot. They asked for a few days to think about this, especially to ascertain if they are the qualified people to lead this program. I assured them that they could take all the time they needed. We closed our meeting by reminding them to let us know their financial requirements too. They agreed to get back to Ed and me by Friday this week.

I emailed Margaret requesting that she notify each of the parishes about the new deaconate program through the February Diocesan newsletter. Father Mike and I reviewed this newsletter that Ed has prepared. The content is as follows, "All Catholics throughout the diocesan are invited to enter the Diaconate program that begins in March and ends in June. Applicants will need to provide a character reference, a letter alleging a clean criminal record by the local police, a letter of recommendation from your parish priest, a copy of your baptismal certificate, a copy of your birth certificate confirming that you are at least thirty-five years of age and a statement of your employment history.

All this information is required by mid-February to make the March 01 commencement date.

## Dinner with the Taylors

Dinner at 7:00 pm was new for me. My stomach is programmed to eat earlier. Paul gave me a cocktail, a strong one, as he welcomed me into his home, He informed me that Simone's house rule is no talking about work during our dinner visit. I was totally OK with that. Maggie's two younger brothers were proudly hovering over their little sister's crib. They will be wonderfully protective. Simone had prepared a "pot au feu", French style casserole of sirloin beef, root vegetables and herbs, a first for me. Her crème brûlée was to die for. After dinner, Maggie woke up her precious little daughter and allowed me to hold her for a photo. She appeared to be a very calm baby. Possible names include Ruth Ann (no nicknames there), Deborah Elizabeth and Daphne Simone. While Simone and Maggie cleaned up, I joined Paul and the two boys to watch the last period of an NHL game between Edmonton Oilers and the Vancouver Canucks.

At 11:00 pm, I received a phone call from St. Jude's Hospital stating that Father Mike had suffered a massive heart attack. Could I could immediately and give him the Sacrament of the Sick and the last rites of the Church? 30 minutes later, I was at his bedside administering the holy oils and the blessings. He was not conscious. He was not going to be the anchor for me that he once was. Am I ready to work alone? No, but I have many assistants with whom I can consult. I slept at Father Mike's that night.

Father in heaven, thank you for the Benedictines, for Ed, the Taylors, their miracle child and their loving and miraculous response to this little girl, for Father Mike. Please help me guide him into a quiet and well-earned retirement.

# Tuesday, February 02
# Scripture study "Amos, the prophet" and The Resolution of the Class Action suit.

Mantra for the day

"This is the day the Lord has made; let us rejoice and be glad" (Book of Psalms, ch. 118, v. 24).

## Scripture Study: Amos the prophet

## Summary of notes:

Who was Amos the prophet?

Amos lived and worked during the reign of King Jeroboam II of Israel (782-758) and the of King Uzziah of Judah (767-738 BCE). Israel, the northern kingdom was comprised ten of the tribes whereas Judah, the southern kingdom, was comprised the two tribes. The original twelve tribes that David had united were now divided into a northern and southern kingdom. Amos lived in Tekoa, a town southeast of Jerusalem in the southern Kingdom. He was a herdsman of sheep and pruner of sycamore trees to support himself. He was not from the priestly class but was called to be a prophet of Israel.

Israel, at that time, was secure from outward enemies and inwardly prosperous. Jeroboam the King was capable politically and militarily; the most successful of the kings of Israel. He expanded Israel's territory at a time when Assyria was pre-occupied with internal matters. He defeated the City of Damascus (a City located in the north) and had control of the main trade route linking Egypt to the nations to the north and the east. Signs of prosperity were common; large mansions, owning a summer and a winter home and the decorating one's home with stone, ivory and other comforts. Israelites became self-indulgent, idle and overly comfortable. Prosperity had produced benefits: pride, selfishness, greed, oppression and moral decay. There was no justice in the land; the poor were afflicted, exploited, even sold into slavery; even the judges were corrupt. Israel at the height of its power and material prosperity, was not able to hear Amos predicting that the destructive power of Assyria's army would become the instrument of God's wrath upon Israel within forty years. The Israelites were approximately 350 years since Yahweh had rescued from the oppressive Egyptians and they had had forgotten the lessons that they had learned in the desert and that they were a pilgrim people.

Message of Amos:

He was sent to Bethel a religious sanctuary in Israel. He announces a judgment chiefly against Israel because of her social injustices, moral degeneracy and apostasy (the abandonment of one's religious commitments). He sees justice and ethical conduct between humans as the foundation of society and maintains that worship by a people whose lives are characterized by selfishness, greed, immortality and oppression is an abomination (wicked or hateful) to God. He warns Israel to change or face the consequences.

Amos condemned the surrounding nations for international crimes as well: Tyre had violated a treaty and Edom had ignored family obligations. Syria had tortured and slaughtered people in Gilead. Philistia had carried many into captivity, selling them into slavery for financial reasons. The Ammonites had murdered women with children in Gilead to annex their land. Moabites had burned the bones of their king.

The focus of Amos was on Israel and its apostasy. God's relationship with Israel was unique and special; not enjoyed by other nations. Since Yahweh had chosen Israelites from the nations, it became the recipient of special favors and privileges.

Israel prided herself on her election but rejected her moral and ethical responsibilities. It was called to be "a holy people", a people of his own possession and special above all the peoples on earth.

Amos also preached that God was particularly incensed that the Israelites could think that they could worship him but behave so unjustly with their fellow Israelites. He insisted that the external practice of religion separated from right ethical conduct was unacceptable to God.

In spite of the destruction to follow, there would be hope. Amos believes that Yahweh will preserve a remnant, a small group of Israelites that will persevere in practicing social justice according to the covenant and be loyal to Him. Yahweh was not a stern God and not demanding a rigid formula of justice. He has a deep affection for His people and in spite of their faithlessness that He has overlooked and forgiven them. Yahweh yearns for their return to Him as expressed in the lament, "yet you did not return to me."

Takeaways:

- Yahweh (God) had a longstanding and a special intimate relationship with the Israelites,
- Amos in criticizing the surrounding nations, teaches that there is a moral code within each of us that demands we acknowledge and follow. Yahweh is the God of all peoples, not just Israel.
- Amos teaches that the practice of religion without being responsible for one's neighbor is unacceptable to God.
- Amos teaches that there is hope. Yahweh's affection for Israel means that compassion and mercy will always overrule justice and retribution.

At 5:00 pm sharp, Peter and I were escorted into Paul's spacious office. Mabel was already seated, looking her usual self-assured. Paul began by saying that he and Mabel had reviewed the terms of the Bishop's committee and while they did not agree totally with all of them, especially about the control of the documentation, they were prepared move on. They were happy that the Bishops and the Diocese were prepared to accommodate the change of the role of women in the Diocese. Paul wanted to know how did the Bishops think that this project would not eventually get into the hands of the press. This will be truly a hot story. But if some group, diocese or whatever requests his help in achieving something similar to what we achieved here, he assured us that he would feel bound by the Provincial Legal code of Conduct for lawyers to assist.

Not sure where this conversation was headed, I signaled to Peter that I was finished. Given the end of a long week, the meeting ended curtly. As I was leaving, Mabel excitedly approached me saying that Susan and her new baby girl would be living with she and Ned while she plans her next move. She is going to introduce Susan and Maggie at the first opportunity. Their mutual interest in legal work and two new babies would make them ideal friends.

I emailed Archbishop Ben that we have dodged a bullet; the Class Action suit has been cancelled before the papers were filed at Court. The men of the parish and my friends in the LGBTQ2S+ and the transgender community have been given the same rights the women have gained. He reluctantly agreed.

I also informed him that Father Joe and his colleagues are analyzing my request to take on the preparation of the future deacons. He quickly wrote back, "How much are their fees?". To which I replied, "still to be worked out". I have also approached them to preach a retreat for the priests of the diocese on Benedictine spirituality. He wanted to know when it was to occur so that he would come too, if invited. I assured him that the Diocese has an open door to him, always. He thanked me again for all my hard work and my love for the Church.

Father in heaven, thank you for your strength, insight and assistance You gave me to follow your will. Thank you for

Archbishop Ben and the Benedictines. As always, please care and protect my family, my friends and my parishioners. Thank you.

## Wednesday, February 03

Mantra for the Day:

"Let nothing disturb you, let nothing frighten you. All things pass. God does not change. Patience achieves everything." (St Teresa of Avila, 1515-1582)

.Thelma emailed me that Chad and Chuck will happily turn the farm into a weekend child care facility for the married couple's weekend. How many children should the boys expect and what are their ages? Please advise of any food allergies or chemical sensitivities. More details to follow.

Ed emailed out our first diocesan newsletter to every parish in the Diocese including the Cardinal and Archbishop Ben. They want to be included in all official correspondence of the Diocese. The newsletter explained that due to recent Court case involving Father Ryan, the financial settlement required by the Court was beyond our current available finances. The Diocesan Financial Committee after careful analyzing the situation, recommended the sale of the Cathedral building and property. While being totally undesirable, there was no other solution. The sale, however, could be a blessing in disguise, as the Cathedral was in need with some major, expensive renovations. Negotiations were underway to rent space in the nearby St. Bonaventure Anglican Cathedral when required for major religious feast days.

To address our dire financial situation, the Diocese has decided to run an annual lottery. The details are still to be worked out. Father Ryan is living in a secured place in a Benedictine monastery never again to harm anyone.

I emailed Margaret asking her to invite all the priests of the Diocese to a special lunch meeting on Tuesday, February 07 in the Cathedral boardroom starting at 11:00 am. I phoned Father Joe and left a message on his voicemail requesting a short meeting ASAP. He replied tomorrow at 10:00 am at their residence.

Father in heaven, thank you for Chad and Chuck, for Ed's wonderful writing skills, the Anglicans for their willingness to share their Cathedral with us and for your many blessings.

## Thursday, February 04
## Meeting with the Benedictines and the Men's Group meeting

Mantra for the Day:

"You who live in the shelter of God, who abide in the shadow of the Almighty, will say to the Lord, 'My refuge and my fortress; my God, in whom I trust. For he will deliver you from the snare of the fowler and from deadly hazards; he will cover you with his pinions, and under his wings you will find refuge; his faithfulness is a shield and a buckler'" (Book of Psalms, ch. 91, v. 1-4).

At 10:00 am, Fathers Joe, Martin and Basil welcomed me into their small apartment/office. After being given a cup of tea (not my usual strong coffee. How do they get anything done?) I reminded them that the Diocese was in short supply of priests available for weekend parish work. I explained the situation concerning Fathers Ryan, Raj, Hildebrand and now Mike. While they were teaching and working in our Diocese for the next five months, could they also fill in on Sundays where there was a need. Father Joe asked for time to consult the Abbot and get back to me quickly.

I emailed Ed to get out a notice to the parishes of St. Francis and St. Joseph of the couples' retreat scheduled for February 20/21 inviting them to sign up and indicate if child care is required.

At 7:00 pm, the St. Francis Rectory boardroom was filled with our usual members of the Men's Club, including Ed Malone. I introduced Ed as the new Diocesan communication director. He received a hearty round of applause. Bill asked for the floor and reported that the snow clearing program was very successful and there is no shortage of members of the community wanting to earn extra money. Fred reported that he, Thelma and Archbishop Ben were leaving Monday for ten days of touring potential sites in Ecuador, Haiti and Peru for the Developing Nations Program projects.

I then informed those present that the Diocese and our two parishes would be formally inviting men and women to consider entering the study program to become deacons. I would also be inviting members of the LGBTQ2S+ community and suspected that Jerome and Raymond would be their candidates. It would to be an on-line course with Saturday in-person classes once a month. The Benedictines had agreed to run the course. Ordination to the deaconate of proven candidates would occur in late June or early July.

I informed the men that due to our difficult financial situation resulting from Father Ryan's court hearing, the Diocesan Financial Committee is recommending the sale of the Cathedral. The sale was finalized for 1.2million and the Diocese will own space for a small chapel in the new building and a new 1400 square foot 2-bedroom, 2-bathroom apartment. Negotiations are nearly complete to rent the nearby Anglican Cathedral for large feasts and events. Fred also informed us that he and

Thelma would be taking the lead on the new Diocesan lottery that is being proposed.

Father in heaven, thank you for the Benedictines, Ed and the members of the men's club and for the quiet day for office work.

## Friday/ February 05
## Cleaning out the Cathedral

> Mantra for the Day:
>
> "O Lord, you have searched me and known me. You know when I sit down and when I rise up; you know my thoughts from far away. You search out my path and my lying down, and are acquainted with all my ways" (Book of Psalms, ch. 139, v. 1-3).

Margaret agreed to supervise the move out from the Cathedral. She rented three large storage lockers for the investments, the relics, the statues and the electric organ. The stained-glass windows would be carefully removed before demolition. It was a sad day as it has been in existence for over 85 years.

Susan Green accepted my proposal and recommended Dr. Jill Wyatt, a well-known psychologist for the married couples' weekend. I emailed Dr. Wyatt of our weekend couples retreat and how important her advice and experience would be to approximately 12 couples who would be attending. The couples would be making presentations as well. I assured her that I hoped this weekend would be interesting for her too.

Father in heaven, thank you as always for Margaret and her efficient ways, the movers who carefully removed our precious

Church items. Thank you for Susan Green and perhaps even Dr. Jill Wyatt. Another one of your special surprises.

## Saturday/Sunday, February 05/06
## Preach "Amos the prophet"

Mantra for the Day

"O Lord, before a word is even on my tongue, you know it completely. You hem me in, behind and before, and lay your hand upon me. Such knowledge is too wonderful for me; it is so high that I cannot attain it" (Book of Psalms, ch. 139, v. 4-6).

### Preach Amos the prophet

*"My dear friends, as always, I thank you sincerely for attending Mass today and including God in your life. I would like to chat with you today about Amos the prophet one of our religious ancestors. He worked as a prophet or teacher from 796 BCE to 742 BCE. He grew up in Tekoa, a small town located a short distance south east of Jerusalem. Like many of these Old Testament prophets, he was not from the priestly class but instead earned his livelihood as a shepherd and as a pruner of sycamore trees, famous for their shade. Israel at that time, enjoyed political security from its large more powerful neighbours. Its location on the major trade routes meant they were wealthy and the signs of their prosperity were large mansions, owning both summer*

*and winter homes and decorating their homes with stone, ivory and other comforts. The Israelites had become self-indulgent, greedy and comfortable. This prosperity produced the negative behaviors of pride, selfishness, greed, moral decay and apostacy. There was no justice in the land: the poor were afflicted, exploited, even sold into slavery; even the judges were corrupt. They worshipped false gods and had forgotten their status and role as a pilgrim people resulting from their relationship with Yahweh. They had forgotten that Yahweh, their special friend and protector identified with the poor and the oppressed as He did with them when they were in Egypt*

*So, Amos was called by Yahweh to go to Bethel, the religious centre in Israel of the northern tribes and to preach that Yahweh is very disappointed and angry. They were in violation of their covenant relationship made at Mount Sinai. They had forgotten that they were a pilgrim people. Amos was so critical in Bethel, that he was told to leave and never to return. Amos further predicted that Israel's enemies such as Assyria, would become God's destructive force in reminding Israel of its covenant responsibilities.*

*Amos had reminded them how Yahweh recued them from Egypt, led them into the desert for 40 years where he guided them, fed them and protected them. Yahweh's relationship with them also demanded that they care and protect one another especially the poor and the vulnerable.*

*The story ends with the Israelites ignoring Amos and in 721 BCE, Assyria captured Israel and carried off a large population of its inhabitants into exile as punishment.*

*Through the sacraments of Baptism, Confirmation and regular attendance at mass we have entered into a covenant relationship with Yahweh, our God who loves us. Like Amos, we are reminded that we are to work for social justice particularly with the poor and the vulnerable. We too are a pilgrim people, journeying through good times and bad. We will encounter deserts along the way when everything will seem difficult, lost and meaningless. This will be an opportunity to turn again to Yahweh, our heavenly Father requesting His guidance, His protection and His love as He did with the Israelites in the desert. Yahweh does not want our church attendance and our prayers if we are neglecting or avoiding the opportunities to be kind and helpful to those around us. Yahweh is attached to the poor, the lonely, the depressed and the sick. Let us keep Yahweh's favorites in our prayers this week."*

## Dinner with the family:

Dinner was a normal noisy, busy family get together. I got to ask everyone a question on how they were. The two nephews are still loving hockey. One niece is into gymnastics and other is into ballet. Sis is teaching Russian literature, her husband is making big money at his investment bank, Brad and Dad are busy too. Mother reported that she and Dad have not felt this good in years thanks to the San Diego holiday. Mother prepared a roast chicken, mashed potatoes,

Brussel sprouts and a rhubarb and custard pie for dessert.

Father in heaven, thank you for another wonderful day doing your work. Sundays are special as the Church family gets together. I pray for the Pope, the Bishops, the parishioners of this diocese, the sick, the lonely and the homeless.

## Monday, February 07
## Day off and Diocesan priest's meeting

Mantra for the Day:

"O Lord, you are everywhere; where can I go from your gaze? Or where can I flee from your presence? If I ascend to heaven, you are there; if I go underground, you are there too" (Book of Psalms, ch. 139, v. 7-8).

At 10:00 am, I welcomed again the priests of the diocese. After an introductory prayer asking for the Holy Spirit's wisdom, I passed out a questionnaire related to assessing their quality of life. Living alone can be challenging and Father Mike and I as your leaders are concerned about you. You are welcome to break up into small groups and discuss the questions. There will be a light lunch served at 11:30 am. Please ensure that Margaret has your completed questionnaires by Friday, February 11.

I received an email from Susan Green confirming that a Dr. Jill Wyatt, a psychologist from Toronto has agreed to join us. They have agreed to attend all the sessions given by the respective married couples on Saturday and to give a lecture on Sunday. Airfare, hotel and car rental will be expensive.

Hopefully, they will share a double room and a rented car for the time that they are here.

To: Archbishop Geoffrey Williams, D.D.
Anglican Archdiocese of Assiniboia
Re: Character reference of Father Raj Patel

Dear Archbishop,

    I have known Father Raj Patel for nearly two years. I met him when I joined this Catholic Diocese. Father Raj has worked in St Thomas, a small rural parish and was well loved by his parishioners and by Bishop Benedict. After a fire that destroyed both the Church and the rectory in St. Thomas, he came to live with me for some months and he was re-assigned to other parish duties and as a chaplain at the local University. Father Raj is known as being very kind, accommodating, hard-working and very intelligent. He would be an asset where he goes.

    He was born and raised in Kerala, India and was one of six children, three boys and three girls. He attended a Jesuit college where he was given an excellent academic education. He has had one year of post graduate studies in world religions at a university in India. During the past year, he approached me concerning his fatigue and depression. I suspect that his heavy parish and university responsibilities have contributed to his extensive fatigue. Unfortunately, this diocese does not deal with fatigue and burnout well. It barely has enough priests to meet the demands of our current parishes. He has recently married to someone he knew from high school. His wife teaches the History of India at a university in Western Canada. He is quite spiritual and looks for ways to make our Christian message attractive to others. If you can find a place for him in your Diocese, I heartily recommend it. Please either email me or call if you have particular questions on this matter. My phone number is 192-455-9087.

Thank you Father for the time to get caught up with my mounting pile of reports to read. Thank you for the opportunity to write a character reference for Father Raj. Thank you too for the priests of this Diocese. Please keep them safe and healthy. Thank you for Susan and Dr. Jill.

Best wishes and good health,
Cameron Walker, parish priest
St. Francis, St Brigid and St. Joseph's Parishes

## Tuesday, February 08
## Scripture study "First letter of Paul to the Corinthians"

Mantra for the Day:

"O Lord, if I travelled to the far horizon, you would find me in a minute as you are already there waiting. Then I said to myself, 'He even sees me in the dark'; in fact, darkness is not dark to you; night or day darkness or light are all the same to you" (Book of Psalms, ch. 139, v. 9-12).

### Scripture study: Paul's two letters to the Corinthians

Who was Paul, the Apostle?

1) Paul (or Saul the name given to him at birth) was born between the year 5 BCE and 5 CE in Tarsus, a Mediterranean city in the Province of Galatia. He was a Roman citizen by birth but was raised in a devout Jewish family. He studied with Jewish scholars in Jerusalem and became a Pharisee, a strict practitioner

of orthodox Judaism. He began to persecute the early Christians by putting them in jail.

2) During a trip to Damascus, he experienced a vision of the risen Christ. He was knocked to the ground and heard a voice speaking to him, "Saul, Saul, why are you persecuting me. He asked, "Who are you, Lord?" The reply came, "I am Jesus of Nazareth, whom you are persecuting". He was blinded for three days, spending them in prayer, taking no food or water, eventually receiving his sight.

3) He became a travelling teacher; he preached "the good news" throughout the Mediterranean even as far west as Spain. He also taught that new Christians, did not have to be circumcised or follow the Mosaic Law (the Torah).

4) Eventually, during a trip to Jerusalem, he was accused of bringing Gentiles into the Temple, forsaking Moses and the Torah and the need for circumcision. The Jewish leaders wanted Paul dead. When attacked by a mob, he was saved by the local Roman tribune, imprisoned in Caesarea and eventually transported to Rome in 60 CE. He was martyred in Rome in 68 CE.

5) Thirteen letters are attributed to St. Paul. But scholars believe that he only wrote the first seven; First Thessalonians, First and Second Corinthians, Galatians, Romans, Philippians and Philemon. His authorship in the remaining six letters is debated. He wrote First Corinthians between 56 and 58 C.E.

Paul's letters:

a) Paul wrote his letters from the major cities at the time where he lived and worked. They were Rome, Alexandria, Antioch of Syria, Ephesus and Corinth. His home base is believed to be Antioch.

b) Corinth was a leading Greek city at the time. It was the capital of the Roman province Achaia and known for its commercial possibilities.
c) Greek society demonstrated high regard for spirituality and aestheticism while also being characterized for the worst vices of hedonism and licentiousness.
d) Paul stayed in Corinth longer than any other place. He lived and worked with Aquila and Pricilla, two Jewish-Christian friends. He supported himself making and selling tents.
e) While he began his time in Corinth preaching to the Jewish population, he changed his focus to the Gentile population after continually being assaulted by the Jewish community.
f) The prevailing Greek's philosophy was based on the body-spirit dichotomy, claiming a superiority of the spirit over the physical (the body). This dualistic thinking led to many divisions in the Corinthian Christian community. These included 1) allegiance to certain members and not others, 2) on celibate versus married life-styles, 3) ostracizing of the poor, 4) the mocking of the teaching of the resurrection of the body, 4) the judging of the authority of the apostles based on external behaviors, and 5) a smug acceptance of basic taboos such as incest.
g) Paul's overall theme is the unity of mankind with our loving Father in heaven and with each other. From this unity flows "the good news". For Paul, "the good news" is that God has given us all a relationship with Him/Her (God is non-binary) and with each other. We are holy neither because of what we have done nor because of who we are, but because our loving Father in heaven has reached out to us. The faithfulness of Abraham and the obedience of Jesus are role models for us to fulfill our relationship with God.

h) The theme of being united with Jesus even in His death and resurrection is a recurring theme in Paul's letters. Being united with Jesus meaning being united in love with all creatures in the Father's family.

Key takeaway: Paul's poetic description of love (First Corinthians, Chapter 13, verses 1-8)

"If I speak with human eloquence and angelic ecstasy but don't love, I'm nothing but the creaking of a rusty gate. If I speak God's word with power, revealing all his mysteries and making everything plain as day, and if I have faith that says to a mountain, "Jump," and it jumps, but I don't love, I'm nothing.

If I give everything I own to the poor and even go to the stake to be burned as a martyr, but I do not love, I've gotten nowhere. So, no matter what I say, what I believe, and what I do, I'm bankrupt without love.

Love never gives up. Love cares more for others than for oneself. Love doesn't want what it doesn't have. Love does not strut, Doesn't have a swelled head, Doesn't force itself on others, Isn't always "me first," Doesn't fly off the handle, Doesn't keep score of the sins of others, Doesn't revel when others grovel, Takes pleasure in the flowering of the truth, Puts up with anything, Trusts God always, Always looks for the best, Never looks back, but keeps going to the end. Love never dies."

Father in heaven, thank you for this special day, a day with St. Paul's words to the Corinthians. While his hymn to love is beautiful, it is very hard to live up to this ideal.

# Wednesday, February 09

Mantra for the Day:

"O Lord, it was you who formed my inner parts; you knit me together in my mother's womb. I praise you, for I am wonderfully made. Wonderful are your works. You know me inside and out. You know every bone in my body; you know how I was made and how I was sculptured from nothing into something" (Book of Psalms, 139 : 13-15).

I emailed Ed asking him to get a second notice in all parish bulletins announcing the deaconate and priesthood training programs. Please explain that this training will allow a successful candidate to assist their parish priests in the delivery of the sacraments and preaching at Sunday Mass. These part-time training programs will begin in early March, so to all those interested, please get you letters of intent to Margaret ASAP. Ed acknowledged my request. I invited he and Elaine to dinner of curries à la Cam.

Dinner with Ed and Elaine was very interesting. Barely in the door, Elaine challenged us on our lack of programs for drug users. "Don't you guys think that saving lives from drug overdoses is a higher priority than cleaning the snow off sidewalks? Or cutting the grass? Or picking up trash? More people are dying from overdoses than from cancer according to her numbers." My curried chicken, brown basmati rice, curried mixed vegetables including potatoes, cauliflower and green beans with a nice Chianti red did not slow her down. Not even some of my mother's butter tarts. By the end of the evening, she seemed to run out of energy, partly due to our suggestion that she take this matter to the local CWA or the Interdenominational Group. I suggested that both groups may be looking for a new project to dig into. PS: my curried chicken and curried vegetables, rice and naan bread were wolfed down with out a comment. I take that as a complement.

Father in heaven, thank you for Ed and Elaine. They add so much to my life and work.

## Thursday, February 10

> Mantra for the Day:
>
> "No eye has seen, nor ear heard nor the human heart conceived what God has prepared for those who love Him"
> (First Letter of Paul to the Corinthians, ch. 2, v. 9).

Simone emailed requesting an appointment for a baptism of their new family member. I phoned her immediately to ask if she considered asking Father Mike, their parish priest to do the baptism. If I was available, I would be happy to just attend. But it is up to you. She replied that Father Mike was saving his energies for celebrating Mass for his parishioners. He regretted that he was too weak and that we should come to St. Francis. I offered her either 1:00 pm on Sunday, February 14 or at 3:00 pm. She requested 3:00 pm

Mabel coincidently phoned to request an appointment to have Susan's baby girl privately baptized. I totally understood the need for a private baptism. I suggested next Saturday or next Sunday afternoons. I was available at both times. It would be a very small group. Mabel has invited her daughters and their families to come. She has also invited Nurse Rita from the local hospital and the members from the CWA. There will be a small family celebration at their home afterwards. She asked if 1:00 pm Sunday was available. We agreed.

At 3:00 pm, my Interdenominational Committee colleagues filed in to the boardroom for our monthly meeting. As usual, they were excited to re-connect with one another. I explained to them all my good news; the approval of the training programs for the deaconate and the priesthood and the married couples' weekend. Joan immediately asked for the floor. Could she and her partner Helen apply to attend the couples' weekend? I said yes of course. I said that we had not heard from the Catholics yet and if there is a low demand and there is space, you both would be very welcome. I will not know until February 17. Joan raised her hand again; could she and Helen be eligible for the deaconate course? Same answer, Joan. Your names are on both lists as of now. After a lengthy debate, it was agreed that the painting of all the buildings in town would provide a bigger bang for our buck and should be pursued. Ed agreed to follow up with the Town Office.

Father in heaven, thank you for my Interdenominational colleagues. They are a breath of fresh air. They respond to me straight up, no Catholic deference.

## Friday, February 11

Mantra for the Day:

"Do to others whatever you would have them do for you. This is the law and the prophets" (Book of Matthew, ch. 7, v. 12).

9:00 am, I phoned Margaret requesting a short meeting and lunch. We agreed to lunch at a new Thai restaurant within walking distance from her office. I spent more time preparing for the married couple's weekend and worrying that none of the couples of the parish have signed up yet.

My meeting with Margaret was calming. She is so organized. As expected, Max looked upbeat to see me. She confessed that she enjoyed working with Ed, our new communications director. I informed her that she has only met one-half of the Ed-Elaine team. Elaine is a nurse who specializes in community health.

I had coffee with my mother and arrived home early with ample time to work on my homily for the weekend.

Mabel emailed me to inform me that her national campaign for women's rights in the Church was now over and she will be returning to the CWA. A nice heads up.

Father in heaven, thank you for another quiet day, lunch with Margaret, hugs from Max, Mabel's return, time with mother and another personal care package from her. Please continue to care for all the people on my list, especially my parishioners, sick family and friends.

## Saturday/Sunday, February 12/13
## Preach: Paul's letters to the Corinthians

Mantra:

"Do not envy the wicked, nor desire to be with them; for their minds devise violence, and their lips talk of mischief. By wisdom a house is built, and by understanding it is established; by knowledge the rooms are filled with all precious and pleasant riches" (Book of Proverbs, ch. 24, v. 1-4).

At 1:00 pm Saturday, Mabel and Ned lead a large group into the Church for the baptism of Susan's daughter, Maria. Ned and Mabel were the god-parents and little Maria slept through the ceremony except for the pouring of water on her forehead. Afterwards at Mabel's and Ned's place, I had a short visit with Susan who expressed her appreciation for all that the parish had done for her. I replied that it was Mabel and the CWA that took the lead in her situation. She also mentioned that she had met Maggie and her baby. She immediately felt that Maggie could be a kindred spirit.

At 3:00 pm, I joined the Taylor family at Father Mike's parish. By comparison to the earlier baptism, they were just the family; Paul, Simone, Maggie, the two boys, James and John and their niece. The boys were given permission to be her god-parents as they felt very protective of her. Another calm baby, named Elizabeth, slept through the ceremony.

I joined the Taylors at their home for a celebratory dinner before returning to St. Francis for a Saturday evening Mass. Maggie informed me that she will continue pursuing her law degree in Montreal once Elizabeth is old enough for day care. She confessed that she is still not sure of God's plan in giving her this little princess, but she is prepared to watch and wait. She is thrilled to have her.

## Saturday/Sunday
## February 12/13

### Preached St Paul's description of love:

> *"Dear friends, thank you for your attendance in Mass today. In our Scripture class last Tuesday, we studied St. Paul's life and his First letter to the Corinthians. Who was Paul the Apostle? While he was called an apostle, he was not part of the original group called by Jesus.*
>
> *Paul, who began life as Saul, was born between the year 5 BCE and 5 CE in Tarsus, a Mediterranean city in the Province of Galatia. He was a Roman citizen by birth but was raised in a devout Jewish family. He studied with Jewish scholars in Jerusalem and became a Pharisee, a strict practitioner of orthodox Judaism. He began to persecute the early Christians by putting them in jail. During a trip to Damascus, he experienced a vision of the risen Christ. He was knocked to the ground and heard a voice speaking to him, 'Saul, Saul, why are you persecuting me. He asked, 'Who are you, Lord?'*

*The reply came, 'I am Jesus of Nazareth, whom you are persecuting.' He was blinded for three days, spending them in prayer, taking no food or water, eventually receiving his sight.*

*He preached "the good news" throughout the Mediterranean even as far west as Spain. He also taught that new Christians, the followers of Christ, did not have to be circumcised, or follow the Mosaic Law (the Torah). Eventually, during a trip to Jerusalem, he was accused by the Jewish authorities of bringing Gentiles into the Temple, forsaking Moses and the Torah and the need for circumcision. The Jewish leaders wanted Paul dead. When attacked by a mob, he was saved by the local Roman tribune, imprisoned in Caesarea and eventually moved Rome in 60 CE. He was martyred in Rome in 68 CE.*

*The key to understanding Paul is seeing that a relationship with our loving Father in heaven and with our fellow human beings as being of upmost importance. A positive relationship with both is vital. Consequently, I would like to slowly read to you Paul's description of love, the basis of good relationships:*

*'Love never gives up. Love cares more for others than for self. Love does not want what it does not have. Love does not strut, doesn't have a swelled head, doesn't force itself on others. Isn't always 'me first,' doesn't fly off the handle, doesn't keep score of the sins of others, doesn't revel when others grovel, takes pleasure in the flowering of the truth, puts up with anything, trusts God always, always looks for the best, never looks back, but keeps going to the end. Love never dies.'*

*This is what love means for us Christians."*

**Family dinner:**

I explained to the family the back stories of my two baptism on Saturday maintaining the confidentiality of the identities of both families. These stories make my work and my life so meaningful. I also gave an overview of the married couples retreat weekend scheduled for next Saturday and Sunday. I explained that Susan Green, a marriage counsellor colleague of Wendy and a Dr. Jill Wyatt from Toronto would be giving talks. To Sis's question as to why such programs were not available in City parishes, I replied that this program was a trial to see if it was viable for other parishes. If it were to fail, I would not have wanted you to have wasted your time. I promised to put her on the next list. I returned home to watch a late NHL hockey game between the Vancouver Canucks and the Winnipeg Jets.

## Monday, February 14
## Day off

### Valentine's Day: a day for lovers

Mantra for the day:

"Love is patient; love is kind; love is not envious or boastful or arrogant or rude. It does not insist on its own way; it is not irritable or resentful; it does not rejoice in wrongdoing, but rejoices in the truth" (First Letter of Paul to the Corinthians, ch. 13, v. 4-6).

Margaret phoned requesting some office time with me. We agreed on Wednesday at 10:00 am but no lunch. I was able to spend the rest of the day reading diocesan correspondence packaged by Margaret around two quick walking trips for Tim

Horton's coffee. I phoned Father Mike to inquire how he was managing. He sounded quite upbeat and happy to hear from me. I asked if I could come by tomorrow for lunch and update him on diocesan news. He agreed. I must visit him every week.

Father in heaven, thank you for this day. It was quiet, peaceful and productive. Keep the Pope, the Bishops, my family and parishioners, sick family and friends, the homeless and refugees in your prayers.

## Tuesday, February 15
## Scripture study: Paul's letter to Philemon

Mantra for the day:

"I am the bread of life, says the Lord; whoever comes to me will not hunger and whoever believes in me will never thirst"
(Gospel of John, ch. 6, v. 35).

### Summary notes: St. Paul's letter to Philemon

Key elements:

1) This letter, the shortest of his letters is officially attributed to Paul.
2) Philemon is alleged to live in Colossae, a small town in south western Turkey.
3) At this point, Christian communities were often comprised of no more than thirty persons. They were meeting in private homes as large church buildings could not be justified or built.
4) Philemon's slave Onesimus had run away. Paul's opinion was that the slave was useless (no reason given). Now however, Onesimus had become a Christian, turned his

life around and was prepared to return to Philemon's service. Slavery was acceptable during this period.
5) Paul beseeches Philemon to accept back Onesimus as he has become a Christian and reformed himself. It is interesting that Paul does not demand that Philemon free Onesimus, but to treat him with love, tolerance and equality.
6) Paul teaches that for Christians, all persons are like brothers and sisters in Christ, whether slave or freeman

1:00 pm, I put together a list of the couples who have signed up for our married couples' weekend. They are Fred and Thelma, Mabel and Ned, Bill and Liz McMillan, Ed and Elaine, Colin and Marion, Jim and Judy, Mario and Isabella, Tom and Ann, Reverend Claire and Hugh, Reverend Joan and her wife, Helen and Jerome and Raymond. Still room for a late comer or two.

I phoned Chad and Chuck and suggested that if the parents are late in indicating to you guys the number of children coming and their special nutrient needs, they should prepare snacks of fruit and vegetables as well as fruit juices. The kids will survive on that. They were very excited to be able to host whatever number of children dropped off.

Susan Green phoned to inquire about food, accommodation and transportation. I informed her that the parish had booked two rooms at the Best Western, one for Jill and one for her for two nights; Friday and Saturday. This hotel is one of our finest. We have booked a rental car for them as well at the hotel. The concierge will advise how to access the car and how to get to the parish. I will have a check for both your airline tickets; please provide the costs. We expect that you will want to return to your hotel Saturday evening. The Hotel has waved the regular departure time

Father in heaven, thank you for another busy but quiet day.

## Wednesday, February 16

Mantra for the day:

"Behold, I stand at the door and knock, says the Lord. If anyone hears my voice and opens the door to me, I will enter his house and dine with him and he with me" (Book of Revelations, ch. 3, v. 20).

At 10.00 am, after being warmly greeted by Max, Margaret announced that she had a wonderful candidate to replace her. There were half a dozen respondents to the ad, but one stood out. Her name is Mabel Armstrong. I nearly fell off my chair. I asked her if she was sure. She replied that Mabel clearly stood out among the candidates. I was more than surprised. She asked if she could phone Mabel and offer the job? I asked for a few days to slowly digest this information. Father in heaven, such a surprise but in another way, it is not a surprise.

Lunch with Father Mike was interesting. He walks very slowly and carefully, using a cane. He does not let his declining health deter him from being well groomed. Over vegetable soup and an egg salad sandwich on multi-grain bread, he listened carefully to my nattering about church life in the Diocese. He perked up when I informed him that Margaret was recommending that Mabel Armstrong replace her in the Diocesan office. We both had a good laugh. My only concern is her notoriety as a CWA member and from her cross Canada crusade. He suggested that we should try to muzzle her as a condition of employment as we have done with Ed Malone. I agreed.

3:00 pm, I joined a meeting in the Town Office to review the plans for the development and expansion of the town. The plans are impressive and full of color and detail. An Open House is planned to invite comments from the town's people.

The January date approval by Town Council has come and gone due to innumerable delays. Good decisions take time.

## Men's Club meeting

The usual group showed up even Ed Malone. The meeting focussed on how the expansion and development would be unfolding. I shared my experience in developing social housing and emergency shelters for both men and women. I encouraged each member to look at investing in real estate development. I advised this group of the plan by the Interdenominational group to paint all the buildings in the Town. There were murmurs and skepticism. Two hours went by quickly.

Father in heaven, why am I so reluctant to hire Mabel. She is extremely competent and well organized; just what we need in this transition period. Is this reluctance revealing my bruised ego? Besides, I would get two for the price of one as Ned will be hovering around Mabel too. Father in heaven, thank you for all that You did for me again today. My life is never boring.

## Thursday, February 17
## CWA meeting

Mantra for the day:

"Holiness consists simply in doing God's will and being what God wants us to be". (St. Thérèse of Lisieux 1873-1898)

After sleeping on it, I emailed Margaret and asked her to offer Mabel the job. I will need someone very competent.

## CWA meeting
## Full house tonight

As usual. Mabel is still getting a lot of attention for her courage and stamina in taking on the Church. Before the meeting got underway, I asked for a private word with her. Removing herself from the group, I asked her if I could announce her new job as Diocesan secretary. She smiled politely and said yes, of course. Mabel led the meeting with the prayer of St. Francis. I announced that Mabel was recently hired as the new Diocesan secretary. The room exploded with cheers and excitement. I then outlined the recent conversation with Elaine about high rate of death of young people from drug overdoses. They agreed to help and I referred them to Elaine for follow-up.

Thank you Father for Mabel and Ned, Elaine's concern for drug users, the CWA, Margaret, Max, family, friends and parishioners especially those in need.

## Friday, February 18

> Mantra for the day:
>
> "Come to me, all who weary and are burdened, and I will refresh you. Take my yoke upon you and learn from me for I am gentle and humble of heart and you will find rest for your souls. For my yoke is easy and my burden is light" (Gospel of Matthew, ch. 11, v. 28-30).

I checked off the components of this weekend; the accommodation, airfare, rental car and expenses for our two guests, Mario's pizza and corona beer for lunch on Saturday and a spicy Chicken burger and sweet potato fries from the new A&W restaurant for Sunday lunch. Tim Horton's donuts and pastries for both Saturday and Sunday. Two full urns of coffee will provide abundant caffeine for those of us so addicted. My weekend homily is on "What makes a marriage Catholic".

Father in heaven, this weekend is very special. Help make it a success in that it will inspire the participants to reflect on the many benefits of their marriage and other relationships and in particular, Your role in all these relationships.

## Saturday/Sunday, February 19/20
## Married Couples Weekend

Mantra for the Day:

"Let us love one another, because love is from God; everyone who loves is born of God and knows God" (First Letter of John, ch. 4, v. 7).

Attendees: Parishioners included Mabel and Ned Armstrong, Fred and Thelma Bartlett, Bill and Liz McMillan, Colin and Marion McNeil, Jim and Judy Truman, Mario and Isabella DeMarco and Tom and Ann McCaffrey.

Special guests: Reverend Claire and Hugh Meadows (Anglican Church), Reverend Joan White and her partner Helen Johnson (United Church), Ed and Elaine Malone and Jerome Nesbit and Raymond LeBois from the Samaritan Club.

Professional presenters: Dr. Jill Henderson, Psychologist; Susan Green, Marriage and Counselor, MSW, RSW.

10:00 am I opened the retreat weekend. I thanked everyone for coming. I invited everyone to get a name tag, get a coffee and pastry and introduce yourself to someone that you do not know. We would start in 15 minutes.

10:15 AM My presentation was to set the table for the talks that were to follow. My presentation focused on what is a Christian marriage or Catholic marriage. This was not new for those of you who have participated in a pre-marriage course; in case you have forgotten, it is the life-long agreement or commitment to your partner to love, to accompany, to protect and to care for them throughout your lives together. It also allows for the safe procreation and secure education of children from your relationship if such were to happen. Families and relationships are schools where we learn how to love. Sounds simple? No, not at all. I also used another analogy that my friends in St. Francis have heard before, that marriage and family life is a school of love. They provide an opportunity where we learn to care for others unconditionally. As God our father loves us unconditionally, we are to love one another unconditionally too. Loving unconditionally is not easy. Juggling the demands of spouse, children, work, friends, and older parents can be both exhausting, confusing and sometimes overwhelming. Your partner is your best source in sorting all this out.

Oh yes, Ed, our incessant note-taker has ordered me to take good notes. So, I will be sitting in a corner writing furiously.

10:30 am Ned and Mabel talked on "If I knew what I know today after 25 years of marriage, this is what I would do differently?" Mabel began by thanking me for organizing this special weekend. She grew up in a warm family. Her father was a successful real estate agent and her mother was a teacher. Academic pursuits were important to her and her siblings even during summer vacations at nearby Moose Lake. Her mother passed on to her the important of the noble profession of teaching. She was destined to study education at university. She met Ned at a family wedding and was impressed by his work ethic. It reminded her of her father's work ethic, but she did not want to marry a salesman. One salesman in her life was enough. She found that sales people have very limited private lives. They are always at the "beck and call" of their clients. Ned also seemed a little nerdy to me, not a turn-on, but he was very pleasant and very persuasive, which was a turn-on. Their best times were their summer dates at Moose Lake. When Ned asked her to marry him, she was unsure. He was six years older whereas her parents were of the same age. Nevertheless, they always seemed to get along well and enjoyed their time together, so she said yes.

They were married three months later and purchased a home in the community. She continued that Ned was away from the family working as a sales representative for a fertilizer company, a large employer in the town. As they had a close relationship, she missed him terribly when he was absent especially when he travelled internationally. She frequently felt sorry for herself when she compared herself to other women friends. She missed his love and affection. She even resented his job and begged him to leave it and find work that would allow him to be at home more. When they calmly looked at their situation, they loved the financial freedom his work provided. Mabel knew that the best part of those years was the money he made and she may not have handled having Ned at home all the time any better if he was earning less money. This income enabled them to take long summer vacations and allowed the girls to bring a friend for company. When their two girls began school, she went back to teaching and was able to cope better with his absences. In preparation for this talk, Mabel discovered that she had many personal regrets for not hiring more people to allow for her and Ned to have more personal time together. She thinks that weekend retreats like this one would have helped her cope better. She concluded by confessing that she did not have a good answer to the question.

Ned began by thanking me for organizing this weekend. He quickly thanked Mabel for remaining married to him in spite of his long absences from home. He admitted to being raised on a farm with two brothers and a sister. They only had a small farm with cows and chickens so his father worked in the city as a postal worker to supplement the family income. He strongly advised us to get a university education to avoid the economic problems of having two jobs.

Ned worked in the insurance business after completing high school to help the family financially as well as farm work on the weekends. After five years of selling insurance, he had saved enough to get to university. Both his brothers and his sister had to do the same. He studied agronomy in Winnipeg at the University of Manitoba for three years and then in Indiana for two years completing a Master's of Science in Agronomy. He met Mabel at a large family wedding before he moved to Indiana.

They corresponded by letter during his studies and he would see her during Christmas and summer breaks. She was bright and well organized. She was always well dressed and seemed to have her life in order. He thinks that he fell in love with her before she fell in love with him.

Ned loved the international travel and found it invigorating but his work demanded considerable evening work. Looking back, the long absences made him feel like an outsider when he returned home. He was sensitive enough to allow the three girls to maintain their schedules and be supportive and thereby not disrupting their routines. Ned now thinks that it would have helped a lot if he had dropped off the girls at one of the grandparent's homes for weekends giving they had time alone. Having computers would have allowed them to remain in daily contact wherever he was.

He believes that he loves her more than she loves him. She blushingly disagrees. He did not have a lot of dating experience and was deeply relieved to receive regular letters from her. He admitted that waiting for and receiving a letter from her was exhilarating. He was socially inept but he made up for this lack by being a good salesman. After graduating, he was hired by an International seed company headquartered in France called Production de Semences. He then finally got up the courage to ask Mabel to marry him. She seemed to take forever to decide but finally agreed. They were married shortly thereafter and moved here where they raised two girls who are married and living in the city.

If he were doing this again, he would hire more child care help that could allow he and Mabel to have more personal time together.

11:00 am Fred and Thelma's talk "How we met."

Fred also began by thanking me for organizing this special weekend. He thanked Thelma for being his greatest blessing. She is so good at many things; being a loving wife, a mother, their banker, their business manager, their chef and their hostess. Her only job left is to find suitable wives for Chad and Chuck. He continued that he was playing junior football and working on the farm with his dad at the time. He played defensive tackle and loved the crushing physical contact. His six-foot four-inch two-hundred-and-twenty-pound frame was ideal for football. He had just met Thelma at a Children's Hospital benefit event. She was representing her bank employer. She was a successful loans officer. His brother and sister were still in high school. Then his dad suddenly died from a heart attack. He was devastated. Thelma helped him through this tragedy and supported him assuming control of the farm and setting up trust funds for the university education of his brother and sister. His brother Dick went on to graduate in civil engineering and Susan graduated in veterinary medicine. They dated for three years in what Thelma felt was like ten years. They would talk for hours about finances and investments. Although no one knew, they used to sneak away to a friend's summer cabin for fun.

Thelma began by recounting that Fred played junior football when they met. He was a big man but was very gentle, protective and respectful. She needed that after having survived two bank robberies. When he finally asked her to marry him after what seemed like a forever dating period, she was so ready. As they were already business partners, this helped their relationship get through the challenges of early marriage and develop a mutually agreed upon routine and the raising of their two boys that are now adults. Her banking and investment background allowed her even today to provide business advice to family, friends and neighbours. Compared to some of their high school friends who married early and who are now divorced, they both felt that their early days of marriage by comparison, were smooth without difficulties or traumas, due in part to their Catholic faith.

11:30 am Bill McMillan spoke next. He thanked me for organizing the weekend. He began by reminding us that Father Cam had ruled out dumb jokes in the talks. Whereas, as an experienced car salesman, he likes to warm up a conversation with a new customer with a goofy joke or two. He then apologized to Liz for being such a big cross for her to bear. She is really a model of love and tolerance.

He grew up in the city, an only child of a female single parent. His mother worked nights as a nurse to be home with him during the day. He learned early how to take care of himself. He was working in a grocery store and going to high school when he first saw Liz. She was stunningly beautiful. He, however, had no time for dating or sports because he needed to support his mother's small income. After high school, he joined the local Ford dealership as a sales trainee and loved the work. By his early twenty's, he was ready to get married but Liz was not. She wanted to pursue training as a nurse so he had to put what Liz called, "his out-of-control testosterone" on the shelf as he waited for her. Her academic ambitions triggered his interest in pursuing Ford's business administration opportunities. They finally got married in their late twenties and Ford Motor Company helped him set up a dealership in the community.

Liz McMillan began; She too grew up in the city. They were a family of five. She had two older brothers. Her parents were considered strong Catholics and believed in volunteering in community organizations. They were well educated and stressed a good education especially for her as their only daughter. Mother always told her that girls had to be twice as good as boys to be equal. When she first noticed Bill, he was working at our local Safeway and staring at her. He packed her mother's groceries and asked if he could carry them to the car. On one occasion, after he returned to the store, my mother asked me if I knew him. I said no as I did not know him at the time. But, he packed our groceries at every opportunity for the next six months until he graduated from high school. Mother was impressed by his friendliness and energy. He asked Liz to his graduation dance and then they became a couple. She said to him that he had to come to Sunday mass with her if they were to date. So, one of their weekly dates was attending Sunday mass at Father Mike's parish. He was anxious to settle down, but she wanted a university education in nursing before marriage. Her parents thought that she should be intellectually, financially and emotionally independent before settling down. She graduated with a Master's of Science in Nursing when she was twenty-six and they got married the next year. She thought the wait was wise as it allowed him to become more established in the Ford Motor Company. Believe it or not, we were virgins when we got married. She concluded by saying that her Catholic faith was a calming and steady influence in her life.

## 12:00 to 12:30 pm
## Lunch

**Mario's Pizza and Corona beer for lunch**

Note to self: thank goodness that I am such a compulsive note taker. These journal entries are full of wonderful detail. Ed will be pleased.

12:30 pm Private time for couples: To answer the question, "Knowing what you know today, how would you have acted earlier?"

1:00 pm: Second talk, "First big challenge": Ed and Elaine Malone began the next talk. Ed spoke first, thanking Father Cam and the St. Francis Church family for welcoming he and Elaine into this faith community. He began his working life at the Toronto Tribune and trying to establish himself as a reputable reporter of city hall news. He was working crazy hours. One day, the editor of the Family section asked him if he would do a feature article on who's who in the local bar scene. He jumped at it, giving him a reason to hang out at the bars 24/7. For the next six weeks, he lived in bars interviewing anyone and everyone on why they came to this particular bar. He was loving it. It was a dream job for a young single guy. One night, a group of nurses came in to celebrate a birthday. He horned in on the party with his tape recorder. Elaine was in the group. While the other four were chatty and cooperative, Elaine was not. She did not want to be part of his so-called research. He was stunned. What is wrong with her? He gave her his business card before she left but she would not reciprocate. He was intrigued. Before the evening was over, one of her nurse friends conceded to give him her phone number. A week later, he phoned and asked her out for dinner with the promise of giving her the first look of my feature article on bars and those who frequent them. She reluctantly accepted. During the course of dinner, she explained that she was a very private person and likes to spend a lot of time alone reading, justifying her reluctance to being interviewed. I was jealous as she seemed so thoughtful and well put together. So, we slowly started to date and were married two years later.

Elaine spoke next. She thanked me and the rest of the group for allowing she and Ed to join this very unusual weekend retreat. She admitted that she is not a Catholic and does not like the way the Catholic Church treats women as second-class citizens. She continued, returning to the topic at hand, when she met Ed, he was doing the feature article on bars. She was working as a psych nurse in a community with a developing drug overdose problem. It was horribly depressing work. Her colleagues were getting sick from the stress and the tragic nature of the work. These young people, between the ages of 15 and 30, were in the prime of their lives but were blamed as emotional failures and totally abandoned by society. While she and Ed had a good life living in Little Italy, an Italian neighbourhood, where the food is to die for, she began to fall apart emotionally. So, Ed, an Easterner and growing up in Ontario, agreed to move west to what Easterners considered the "hinterland". She was able to find work at our local hospital and Ed as the editor of the local newspaper. They love the community. They are close enough to the city in the event they need something that our community cannot provide. She concluded by thanking us again for this wonderful opportunity.

2:00 pm: Third talk, "What our 30's brought us": Jim and Judy Truman were next; Jim began thanking Father Cam; he grew up on a farm five miles from town. His parents were very ordinary people, hard-working but happy. He was an only child and happy to move into town after high school. He joined Home Hardware twenty years ago. He met Judy at an annual barn dance in Coburn, a tiny village an hour south of town. She was very pretty, a great dancer and very energetic. He danced with her every dance she allowed him to. Before the evening ended, he asked to drive her home but she refused as she came with another girl friend and they had promised to ride home together. She did give him her phone number. In an effort to be "cool", he waited a week before he called her. When he finally did, she asked him what took him so long. We were twenty when we married. He took over the small family farm five years ago when his parents were too ill to carry on. They just plant grain crops. They have one child, Suzanne, a twelve-year-old girl going on twenty-five. In response to the question, what did living the 30's bring them, three things stand out for him; first that his life was not going to be very different from his parent's life; a lot of work. That was very depressing until once they got their heads around it. Second, growing up as an only child, he wanted to have four children but medically this was not to be. At the birth of our daughter Suzy, the gynecologist discovered uterine cancer and with Judy's permission, removed her uterus. They were blessed as it was in the early stages and Judy is now cancer free. Third, during this cancer scare, Jim begged God to save Judy's life and He did. He is truly grateful for Judy, Suzy and their life together and he thanks God every day for them. He is a better Catholic today because of his 30's. In his case, the fear of losing Judy helped him realize the importance of his Catholic faith.

    Judy spoke next: the lives of Jim's and Judy's paralleled one another. She grew up on a farm. She loved farming. They moved into town so that she and my brother could get a good education, but she really missed the animals. She was forever bringing home stray cats and begging her mother to allow her to keep them. Her mother only agreed if they slept outside in a little shed in their backyard. Mother thought that they needed their independence to hang out with other cats. After high school, her parents had saved up enough money for each of them to go to university. She chose to spend her tuition money on travel to the disappointment of her parents. She flew to France where she was hired by a Parisian family as a nanny. She was given board and room, the equivalent of $50.00 a week and a return plane ticket if she lived in, cared for the three children, three, six and nine years old and took them to and from school. She lived three years with this family. She learned to speak French, loved Paris and the exciting fashions, but missed her family. French men generally scared her. They were very self-assured and too seductive for a person like her. When she met Jim, he seemed so comfortable after all the hustle of Paris. The thirties were a wakeup call for her. She had a cancer scare, they have a lovely precocious daughter Suzanne and Jim is still the same sweet, hardworking, reliable man that she married. Like Jim, she is very grateful to God, to the parish and the community.

2:30 pm: Fourth talk, "But then came the 40's": Mario and Isabella Demarco were scheduled for their 10-minute talk;

Mario began by saying that they own Mario's Pizza but they serve much more than pizza. They are currently expanding their menu to provide Italian dining in the Emilia-Romagna tradition. This region of Italy is famous for its prosciutto di Parma created in Emilia and the king of cheeses Parmigiano Reggiano. It will cater to dining in or take out. We will institute a growing trend in restaurant dining called BYOB, meaning bring your own bottle of wine. Please tell your friends.

The 40's for Isabella and I were a mixed blessing; good news was that their two children, Mark (14) and Stella (12) were old enough to work in the restaurant. Ruth has always been our accountant. The business is a family affair. Our business has also grown with the growth of the town. The bad news was that his parents were in their 80's and need a lot of care and support. Emotionally, their situation can stress them out. He thanks God twice a year, Christmas and Easter for his many blessings.

Isabella began by saying that some of the ladies here know her from the CWA and her need to say it like it is. She was anxiously waiting for a discussion about sex in marriage. Nick chimed in, tomorrow, my Love. She continued that Italian men, in her family have a distorted view of women. They are supposed to act like the Virgin Mary, the mother of Jesus one the one hand during the day and like a hooker in bed at night. Mario interrupted Isabella to publicly thank her for being such a saint and sleeping with him. Like Mario said, Isabella believes that have had a very good life in this community. Her problem is her mother; she is in her late 80's, has an untreatable brain tumor and is allergic to most pain medicine. She prays that God will take her every day. Watching her struggle on her own in the city and knowing the pain she lives with, she would like to suggest to her a doctor assisted death but it is against the teachings of the Church. I know about Father Cam's wife Wendy who chose to end her life on her own terms, but she wants her mother to have a Church burial and to be buried in their family plot. She asked for everyone's advice and she was glad Father Cam was able to hear all this. Note to self: I must have a follow-up visit with Isabella.

3:00 pm Tom and Ann were next. He too thanked me and the other couples for this very unusual retreat. He turned to Isabella and answered her question as to why Catholics don't talk about sex. He thought it was like the subjects of religion, death and taxes that one is not supposed to talk about. Quiet laughter. He owns the pharmacy in town. Like the Hansen's, they live a very good life in this community. The cross that he and Ann carry and she will also speak about it next, is a growing problem today. They had four beautiful girls, one of which died as a result of an overdose from contaminated opioids. Cathy, our eldest worked in the pharmacy when she wasn't either at school or playing basketball. A year ago, she sprained her ankle that seemed to take forever to heal and started stealing drugs from the pharmacy to combat the pain. Six months ago, she took one of our cars to the city on a Friday night and never returned. Her dead body was found abandoned in a lane and the car stolen. The autopsy revealed both oxycontin and amphetamines in her blood. So, the 40's are for them a mixed blessing; self-recrimination, self-blame for not treating the early little signs seriously. He blames himself for this tragedy. He often asks myself and God, why him? Why them? Are they bad people?

Ann began that she thought that she and Tom had the perfect life. Two good jobs, she worked part-time at the public library allowing her to be at home for the girls, four bright beautiful girls and small-town living. As Tom struggled with his regrets and self-recriminations, she was in a different space. She thinks that they took their good life for granted and thought it would just continue to flourish. They were living with blinders on. Perhaps, they could have prevented this loss. She also asks God what she is supposed to learn from all this pain. God has been slow to answer. But perhaps she already knows the answer but just does not like it. Sorry all you good people, but their 40's have been a challenge. She also has great hope for the future.

## 3:30 to 4:00 pm
## Private time for couples

## 4:00 pm Review schedule for tomorrow

I reminded everyone that tomorrow, we continue our retreat with talks by Susan, a marriage counselor and Dr. Jill, a psychologist. We will see you here at 1:00 pm.

I invited Susan and Jill for a light dinner at the rectory. They knew that I had a 7:00 pm mass in the Church. Over Mother's chicken noodle soup, we recapped the talks and commented on the warmth and candor of the couples who spoke today. I assured them that I had not screened or edited their short talks.

Father in heaven, thank you for today. This work of supporting family life gives me such energy and joy. It is truly the core of my work. Thank you for today.

## Saturday Mass/Sunday Mass:
## Preach Married Love

Mantra for today:

"See what love the Father has bestowed on us that we may be called the children of God. Yet we are". (First Letter of John, ch. 3, v. 1).

*"My dear friends, as some of you know, we are having the first married couple's weekend in St. Francis. Eleven couples are spending this Saturday and Sunday focussed on their marriage. The couples themselves are giving the talks and are joined by social worker and a psychologist specializing in keeping marriages and families together. My words today will focus on what is a Catholic marriage and highlight the words from the prophet Hosea.*

*But first, God, our loving father wants to be a part of your life, your marriage and your relationship. This Father, however, is the only third party allowed in a marriage. I do not need to remind you that having a lover while one is married is a recipe for disappointment and failure, that can sadly lead to divorce. Having God our loving Father as a member can strengthen your relationship, especially when the going gets rough. It is during the challenges of a marriage where God the Father can strengthen, support and carry both parties.*

*Hosea is an Old Testament prophet who taught between 786 BCE and 746 BCE. He was one of a group of prophets active during that time. It was a period of economic growth and political stability for the Israelite people. In spite of these good times, there was political corruption, oppression of the poor and idolatry, the worship of false gods. Israel's behavior was in violation of its covenant with God (Yahweh). At Sinai, the covenant specified that God was Israel's only God and Israel was a special people to Yahweh. Abandoning the covenant was wrong.*

> *Covenant relationships are a major theme in the Old testament. God entered into a covenant relationship with Noah, Abraham, Moses and the Israelites at Sinai and with David. Hosea's primary message is that God and the Israelite people have a covenant relationship. Covenant love entails a bond of love and trustworthiness. Hosea uses marriage to explain a covenant relationship.*
>
> *In this unique book of the Old Testament, God wants Hosea to love a woman. Hosea is commanded to go and find a woman guilty of adultery. She is unnamed. The woman is ordered to cease practicing as a prostitute but live separated from Hosea. The period of separation will spark a contrite heart on her part. In spite of her failings, Hosea does not abandon her. In spite of Israel's failures, Yahweh does not abandon her either in spite of getting furiously angry and threatening all kinds of punishments. Nor are we allowed to abandon our unfaithful partners.*
>
> *Hosea holds out hope for both victims of injustice as well as perpetrators of evil. All are invited to return to Yahweh, to experience this face of compassion and healing. Hosea presents the most accurate image we humans have of our God of mystery, it is of compassion."*

Sunday 1:00 pm: "What research tells us about what behaviors work and those that do not work in a marriage relationship",

This talk was given by Susan Green, MSW Clinical therapist; I introduced Susan explaining that she was a close friend of Wendy, my deceased wife and me before I became a priest.

Susan: Thank you Cam for this opportunity to share with you and your parishioners my work and my research on marriage. Being out front, I am not a Catholic. I have known Cam from his previous career as developer of affordable housing and women's emergency shelters. Everybody admired and loved Wendy and Cam. They were a wonderful couple, kind and hospitable. She was a big women's advocate. She was critical of Catholic priests who advised female parishioners to remain in abusive marital relationships. Her death was a horrible shock and even today, many of her friends still cannot believe she is gone.

But, the topic that I have been asked to speak on is "What human behaviors work and what are those that do not work to maintain a happy married and family life?" According to Dr. John Gottman, a well-respected psychologist working in Seattle, there are four big ones; 1.) being defensive when challenged about something, regardless if you are right or wrong, 2) criticism is deadly. Do not criticize you partner/spouse or your children. Rule of thumb: never use the word "you" in a sentence. Such sentences usually can become accusatory. 3) Contempt; having contempt in a relationship is a quick way to get to divorce court. 4) Stonewalling or the refusal to talk about a subject. This is also called the silent treatment. Dr. Gottman has researched communication patterns in couples and families for many years in his Seattle clinic. Then there are the four irritating communication techniques: 1) giving your partner unsolicited advice; 2) correcting your partner's statements or sentences; 3) looking bored or off into space when they are taking to you; and 4) ignoring them or acting like they do not exist.

Susan talked about a fifty-year-old male client, professional engineer whose wife walked out with their three children a year ago. She gave them each a fictitious name; Paul and Mary. After living in a bar for six months, Paul arrived at my office door wanting me to get his wife and children back. I contacted his wife and inquired if she would consider participating in joint counselling. No, she was not interested in counselling with her husband but agreed to individual counselling for herself. Over the course of months of weekly counselling sessions with this woman, I learned again that marriage does not always suit women. There can be an imbalance of power in male-female relationships; men make more money doing the same work than women do and have more power and prestige in our society. When women get married, they thought they wanted to have children, a nice home and become a homemaker because that is what their mothers did. The world has changed. Women are now as well educated, as professional and as interested in business as men but they are still not treated as equal. Women can carry a resentment of their husband or even of men without fully understanding why. This imbalance can cause conflict and stress in a relationship.

Getting back to Paul and Mary, I doubt if they will ever get back together. Why, because Paul wants his old wife back. He still has not accepted the fact of that the marriage is over. She has changed and he has not.

We are learning that women are better multi-taskers than men. Women have babies, cook, clean, iron, chauffeur kids to school, nurture and counsel their children through their challenging growing up years, manage household finances, drive tractors and combines on farms. They do whatever needs to be done. Whereas men would struggle with this level of multi-tasking. So, you men, look again at your partner and realize what an asset or gift you have in your wife. She is your most precious commodity. Please treat her like it. So, based on that, I believe that the following will enhance your marriage: 1.) treat her like your most precious possession; not like a fragile flower. 2.) help her as she carries out her tasks; 3.) take the initiative doing household tasks without being asked; 4.) take the initiative in the kitchen, take a cooking course together; 5.) treat the marriage as a 75-75 partnership where everyone gives more than their share. 6.) phone her or communicate with her during the morning or afternoon to inquire how her day is going. 7.) spend 30 minutes at the end of the day having one on one time with her. 8.) learn to accommodate her differences and her up and down emotional-biological make-up; 9.) allow for change in your lives; 10) encourage her to develop herself, her talents and her abilities. There is a big payoff if you do. She thanked everyone for their patience. She concluded that she would be around for the rest of the day for questions.

2:00 pm: Susan Green introduced Dr. Jill Wyatt the next speaker by describing her, in her opinion, as the best professional psychologist she knows. Her subject is "What does science tell us about our sexual selves". She not only teaches but has practiced for fifteen years in Toronto. She has written and published fifteen articles on marital sexual disfunctioning. Please welcome Dr. Wyatt.

Dr. Wyatt began by thanking everyone for the warm welcome and Father Cam. She loved the Italian lunch as she lives in an older Italian neighbourhood in Toronto where she has enjoyed Italian food, the culture and the language. She continued that she had read in the Toronto Tribune about two clerics in Western Canada and wondered who they might be. She confessed that she had quietly asked Fred, who confirmed that their former Bishop Ben and Father Cam were the culprits. Don't worry, your secret is safe with me.

For the record, she admitted that she is a practicing Catholic and married and thus has a good idea of your marital and sexual daily challenges. We are sexual beings, but we are also physical, emotional, intellectual and spiritual beings. How do we balance these important parts of ourselves with our marital partners?

She began with what textbooks call sexual stages in a marriage and she referred to the scientific work by Dr. Masters and Johnson. Couples in their 20's deal with adolescent energy caused by a high level of testosterone. The goal is as much sex as possible. The male wants to please his partner. In the 30's, it is a very busy stage with the focus is on babies, establishing a home and the finalizing career choices. With the 40's come the first signs of erectile disfunction in men also known as not being to either have an erection or maintain one like they did in their 20's. In his mind, a young man becomes an old-timer as he starts to experience prostate problems, have worries and puts on stomach weight. The male in his 50's, wonders if an affair might re-assure his fragile masculinity. In the 60's and beyond, men can begin to achieve pleasure from his wife's pleasure and they search for different methods of love-making.

Regarding women, it is sad to report, that women, for some unknown reason, have not been the subject of extensive research into their sexuality as men have. The main sexual problem for women is frigidity where they cannot get aroused or even become interested in sexual intercourse. So, ladies, you are still a closed book. If you are experiencing sexual problems, visit your gynecologist first as those problems may have be a medical solution.

As we move into our late adult period, the light at the end of the tunnel for an aging marriage is mutual sexual stimulation. Being sexually active, as we age, can be challenging as men become impotent and women cannot get adequately aroused for intercourse, thinking that their sex lives are finished. In spite of these obstacles, you do not stop being sexual beings. Touching, hugging, kissing and nakedness can be a new adventure in love-making. This can be comforting to one another as you face the challenges of aging.

One solution is the purchase of sexual toys such as a vibrator. She advised that sex shops sell them and can also be purchased even on line. She continued that she had recently read an interesting news clip of a French company that markets a wide variety of these devices. Their motto is "Plaisir au sac" loosely translated as pleasure in your purse. They argue that every older couple or mature woman should have such a device. They can be particularly valuable for widows or women living alone. Growing older means that we do not have the same sources of pleasure that we used to, so we need to improvise. There is a table at the back of the hall that has many different types. They are not for sale but only for information. I understand that we will have a Q. and A. after a short coffee break. Thank you all for your attention.

3:00 pm: I chaired the Q. and A. period. Fred asked for the use of anonymous written questions. Everyone agreed. After a short break for the distribution of paper and pencils and time to write:

Q: Susan, can you please tell us some stories of Father Cam's days before he became a priest?

A: Giggling, yes, of course, we partied with them. They were a fun couple. They used to organize weekend parties at a cabin they rented.

At that point, I became uncomfortable.

She went on to describe in detail the parties that she attended at this cabin and that the nude midnight swims were truly special to my embarrassment and everyone's laughter.

Finally, she concluded that she had embarrassed me enough and I had been a good sport about it.

Q: Next question: Susan, thank you for wonderful talk. How do you get our husbands away from watching sports on TV and talking?

A: I suggest taking courses together; they can include cooking, a history course or learning a language like Spanish that could make your vacations more interesting and it is also good for the brain. Being companionable is a very important habit to develop as you get older.

Q: My husband likes to flirt with younger women and is not even aware of it. What do you suggest, Susan?

A: I suggest marriage counselling. Seeing a marriage counselor is like taking your car to a mechanic for a regular check-up. It is preventive maintenance that both cars and marriages can benefit from. Dr. Jill, do you have anything to add? Thank you, Susan, if I were the questioner, I would recommend first, having her husband checked out for early prostate problems and secondly, check his weight and go to exercise classes together. If there are no classes in your local, purchase a stationery exercise bike and put it in front of the TV. There are very good exercise programs on TV. Exercise is a good way to avoid becoming sedentary as we age.

Q: Can one ever be too old for sex, Dr. Jill?

A: The short answer: never, never. We can be sexually active up to the time of our death.

Q: My husband suffers from extreme modesty. I am German and our family loved nudity, but he is the opposite. Dr. Jill, what do you suggest?

A: I suggest therapy to discover what the concern is. Therapy is a safe and confidential method of addressing and eliminating all kinds of fears.

Q: My husband has an incessant need to correct me in public. I keep telling him that our conversations do not need to describe situations with absolute accuracy. We are not talking about money but people's thoughts and behaviors. Your suggestions please, either Susan or Jill?

A: Susan, that is a communications problem. I refer you to my talk and Dr. Gottman's things to avoid. If this is a persistent problem, I suggest a few sessions of counselling to assess if there may be some type of deep-seated hostility. Jill? She said that she had nothing to add.

Q: Why does my husband tease me in public and embarrass me? Jill responded that she thought it was a way a competitive husband could get back at you. Another example of the need for counselling.

4:00 pm: Conclusion and evaluation.

I thanked everyone especially Dr. Jill and Susan. I asked everyone to give the two speakers a big round of applause. I then thanked the attendees especially those who gave talks of such a personal nature, the Demarco's for catering and Chad and Chuck Bartlett for organizing the child care for these two days. Tomorrow, we will realize this weekend as a most memorable one. Please email me your evaluations.

**Dinner with the Family**

Dinner with family focussed on Dad's retirement from the business. He is now 75 and has persistent heart and lung problems. His mind is still sharp and there are no early signs of dementia. The discussion considered on renting a house in a warm climate for the coldest months of the winter. Mother expressed her desire to have her grandchildren around her as much as possible. Sis, being a teacher, would only be available during the Christmas break whereas I would not be available at Christmas time. My brother agreed with Sis that running the building trades business on his own, would also restrict his holidays too. The parents both expressed that they would be fine this year having had a lovely time in San Diego after Christmas.

Father in heaven, thank you for helping to make the couples weekend such a great success. Thank you for the helpers, the child care guys and girls. It succeeded beyond our expectations. Thank you for my parents, my siblings and nieces and nephews and please keep them in your warm embrace.

## Monday, February 21
## Day off

Mantra for the Day

"In the twilight of life, God will not judge us on our earthy possessions and human successes, but on how well we have loved." St John of the Cross (1542 -1591)

I received emails from both Susan and Jill thanking us for the special weekend particularly our western hospitality. The hotel rooms were great, the car functioned well and they have arrived home safely.

I reviewed the evaluations from the eleven couples. All participants learned a lot and made some good relationships from the experience. The only negative point was that there was not enough time to hear from all the couples, especially the two gay couples. The diocese should offer this experience to all the members of the diocese.

I had a phone call from Isabella requesting an appointment. We agreed to meet at Tim Hortons on Tuesday at 3:00 pm.

## Tuesday, February 22
## Scripture study: Paul's letter to the Philippians and drive to the Monastery

Mantra for the Day

"Remember that the Christian life is one of action; not of speech or daydream. Let there be few words and many deeds and let them be done well." (St Vincent Pallotti, 1795 – 1850)

### Scripture study: Paul's letter to the Philippians

1) Philippi was a Roman city located in Macedonia (in what is today known as northern Greece). It was situated along a major Roman military and trade route at the time called the Via Egnatia and a short distance from the port city of Neapolis.
2) This letter was written between 55 and 57 CE.

3) Key message: Our relationship with Jesus who out of obedience to His heavenly Father, died and was raised from the dead and He has freed, delivered and rescued us to pursue a different lifestyle from those who do not know him. This relationship with Jesus is an opportunity and is a strength, sharing in the power of God our Father. This belief has an energy to it. The message of the cross according to Paul is one of the greatest human mysteries. It is the center of the gospel message. Suffering is valued if it is aligned on Jesus' suffering.
4) Our relationship with God our loving father involves two components; the first, the worship and obedience to God following in the footsteps of Abraham and of Jesus and second, loving one another.
5) Chapter 2, verse 1-11 highlights the basic of Paul's teaching to the Philippians: "Do nothing from selfish ambition or conceit, but in humility, regard others as better than yourselves. Let each of you look not to your own interests, but to the interests of others. Let the same mind be in you that was in Christ Jesus, who, though he was in the form of God, did not regard equality with God as something to be exploited, but emptied himself, taking the form of a slave, being born in human likeness. And being found in human form, he humbled himself and became obedient to the point of death, even death on a cross. Therefore, God also highly exalted him and gave him the name that is above every name, so that at the name of Jesus every knee should bend in heaven and on earth and under the earth, and every tongue should confess that Jesus Christ is Lord to the glory of God the Father."

At 3:00 pm, Isabella and I met at Tim Hortons. She began by thanking me for organizing the married couples weekend and said that she found it very informative and supportive. But then she quickly turned the subject to her mother. Realizing how painful it was for her, I re-assured her that her mother would receive a Christian burial at St. Francis if she chose to die in dignity with the help of physician. Relieved, she thanked me, shook my hand vigorously and stated that she had to get back to help Mario at the restaurant.

Father in heaven, thank you for this class on St. Paul and his letter to the Philippians

## Wednesday, February 23
## A Day off

> Mantra for the day
>
> "Create in me a clean heart, O God, and put a new and right spirit within me. Do not cast me away from your presence, and do not take your holy spirit from me" (Book of Psalms, ch. 51, v. 10-13).

Mabel emailed me requesting a short meeting in the Diocesan office at 10:00 am tomorrow. Margaret and Max (of course) will in attendance. She also invited me to dinner tomorrow, Thursday evening. Susan would be cooking. I agreed to both.

At 3:00 pm sharp, my Interdenominational colleagues were waiting at my door. As usual, we were all excited to see one another. Ed, Claire and Joan expressed high praise for the married couples' weekend. Ed reported that the Town Office would like to take the coordination of the house painting program. Accessing private property, buying paint in bulk and getting agreement of the individual property-owners would be much easier for the Town Office to manage. Ed assured everyone that this committee will be fully involved in the actual painting. He also mentioned that Elaine, his wife the nurse, was very concerned about the growing problem with young people dying from drug overdoses. He inquired if this committee would lend its support for this noble cause. They unanimously agreed and asked Ed to invite her to our next meeting in March.

Father in heaven, thank you for introducing me to these special friends of mine. They are such a breath of fresh air.

## Thursday, February 24

Mantra for the day

"Have mercy on me, O God, according to your steadfast love; according to your abundant mercy blot out my errors and omissions" (Book of Psalms, ch. 51, v. 1).

10:00 am I entered the Diocesan offices to be greeted by Max, Mabel and Margaret. After listening to Mabel describe her responsibilities, I was very pleased again to welcome her into this special work. I explained the code of silence required by the Vatican on the deaconate program and any future innovative programs in the diocese. Then I asked her how she would handle inquiries from the CWA membership across Canada about the outcome to her class action suit. She confessed that she has contacted the national office of the CWA and advised them that she is unable to discuss it publicly as a requirement of her new employment. She hoped that she could talk about it eventually. In the meantime, she requested patience and understanding of the membership regarding this matter. I was pleased and satisfied by her answer.

## Dinner at Mabel and Ned's home

This was a very pleasant visit. Mabel had warned me that Susan was cooking for this dinner and beware. I arrived at 5:30 pm wishing to spend time with Susan's baby. I was met at the door by Ned who was carrying Baby Maria who was sound asleep. To Ned's offer of a cocktail, I requested diet coke alluding to my slow weight gain and tight pants. Susan served a delicious baked chicken lasagna with mixed vegetables comprised of carrots, cauliflower and green onions. I was very impressed. When I asked her where she learned her cooking skills, she replied that Isabella, the woman she lived with during the past year was a very good cook and was happy to teach her. She volunteered that she has completed a legal secretary course and would be looking for work. I turned to Mabel and asked if Paul's legal firm were looking for more staff. She promised to talk to him the next day.

Father in heaven, thank you for this day with Mabel, Margaret, Max, Ned, Susan and Maria.

## Friday, February 25
## Office Work

Mantra for the day

"Happy are those who consider the poor; the Lord delivers them in the days of trouble. The Lord protects them and keeps them alive; they are called happy in the land. You do not give them up to the will of their enemies. The Lord sustains them on their sickbed; in their illness you heal all their infirmities" (Book of Psalms, ch. 41, v. 1-3).

Father in heaven, thank you for a quiet day and time to catch up on items that I have either postponed or neglected. As always, I ask you to care for sick family and friends, the homeless and refugees.

## Saturday/Sunday, February 26/27
## Preach Paul's letter to the Philippians

Mantra for the day

"Do not worry about your life, what you eat or what you will drink, or about your body, what you will wear. Is not life more than food and the body more than clothing. Look at the birds of the air; they neither sow nor reap nor gather into barns and yet your heavenly Father feeds them. Are you not more important than they? And can any of you by worrying add a single hour to your span of life?" (Gospel of Matthew, ch. 6, v. 25-27).

## Preach: St Paul to the Philippians

*"Dear friends, to begin, I would like to begin by thanking you for coming to Mass today. The subject of my chat with you today is St. Paul and his letter to the Philippians. Philippi was a community situated in what is today known as Greece. He visited it on both his second missionary trip (between 49 CE and 52 CE) and his third missionary trip (Between 52 and 57 CE). It is also thought that he wrote the letter to the Philippians from Ephesus where he spent three*

*years preaching and supporting himself, working as a tent maker.*

*His main message to the Philippians is humility. He begins by requesting that they do nothing based on selfish behavior or conceit but in humility regard others as better as yourself. He continues by asking each of them to not look out for your own interests but for the interests of others.*

*Be of the same mind as Jesus, who even though He was God the Father's son, sharing in His divinity, He did not demand equal treatment. Jesus emptied Himself being born as a helpless infant of Mary and Joseph. He humbled himself, becoming obedient to His Father in heaven, even to the point of death, a horrible death on a cross. Crucifixion in those days, was reserved for slaves, criminals and those with no status.*

*Therefore, God the Father raised Him up from the dead and has now exalted Him above every name and person. Jesus is our model of loving behavior."*

## Dinner with the family

Mother's dinner as usual was special. She served baked salmon, a vegetable lasagna with asparagus and baby carrots and a Caesar salad. She wanted to know if I was getting enough sleep. I tried to assure her that I was. Sis chirped in that I look as if I had aged ten years. What was I watching too much late night T.V. Those late-night talk shows can be addictive. Mother came to my rescue asking my sister to leave me alone. My parents looked so much better after their winter break.

Father in heaven thank you for another wonderful weekend at St. Francis, St. Brigid and St. Joseph Parishes. Thank you for my family who keep me humble when I take myself too seriously. XO

## Monday, February 28
## Day off (Ha)

Mantra for the Day

"The Lord delivers the needy one who calls, the poor and the one who has no helper. He has pity on the weak and the needy and saves the lives of the needy" (Book of Psalms, ch. 72, v. 12-13).

While I had no appointments, I spent considerable time with Father Joe and his brother Benedictines, answering questions related to the deaconate program that would be starting very soon.

Father in heaven, thank you for the Benedictines. You are so good to us. They are so good to us too.

# March report from the Diocese of Carthage to the Pope, Vatican Officials and the Canadian Bishops

1) The Deaconate Program:

   Initial applicants who have met all the requirements include Colin and Marion McNeil, Ned Armstrong, Helen Jones and her wife, Melody Summer, Jerome Nesbit and his husband Raymond LeBois, Liz McMillan, Ed and Elaine Malone from St Francis, Simone Taylor from St. Mike's and representatives from fifteen parishes out of forty parishes.

   The March instruction focussed on the sacraments of baptism and confirmation. There were three online sessions studying the biblical origins of these sacraments especially the role of water as a healing, life-giving and cleansing element. There was a one-day class for hands-on teaching of the two sacraments.

2) Diocesan Pastoral Council:

   Ms. Mabel Armstrong has recently been hired as the new Diocesan Secretary and Office Manager. She, with the assistance of Ed Malone, the Diocesan Communications Director are getting newsletters out monthly to all parishes. The Council received a request to allow the United Church parish to rent space in St. Francis. They are too small a congregation to support their church building. The Anglican Church is already renting space at St. Francis. This matter has been referred to the St. Francis Parish Council.

3) Diocesan Financial Committee:

This Committee is reviewing all the maintenance plans for all the properties in the Diocese. The Committee has hired a local engineering company to review these plans and recommend a long-term maintenance plan for the Diocese. This is aimed at keeping our insurance costs in line and avoiding costly fires, claims from and damages to other people's properties. The Committee reported that the Court and the respective families had been paid in full stemming from the Father Ryan court case. There were no other pending financial obligations.

4) Diocesan monthly priest's meeting:

The priests of the Diocese meet the second Wednesday of the month for both study and reflection. We reviewed the results of satisfaction survey of the priests in the Diocese. The major concerns include the aging of the priests in the Diocese and the lack of vocations to the priesthood; the sexual abuse scandals of women and children; the diminishing moral authority of the Church; and the inconsistent communication between the Bishop and the priests of the Diocese. Generally, their level of satisfaction is high when they are being useful especially in celebrating Mass, distributing the sacraments, preaching, helping members of their parish to find Christian spirituality and feeling that they are part of the community.

When asked about the Church allowing married men or women or gays to become deacons and priests, there was general acceptance for men but less (but still a majority) for women and gay transgender priests.

Other concerns included losing their Cathedral, the absence of a Bishop and a feeling that things are changing too fast in the Church.

I asked all the priests present to be particularly supportive of the new Deaconate program especially if you have a candidate in the current program.

5) St Francis Parish Council:

The Parish Council received a request from Reverend Helen Jones and the United Church to rent space for their small congregation and is prepared to accommodate them provided they agree to the similar conditions that the Anglicans have. Ned and Mabel Armstrong have agreed to follow up with Helen and her parish committee.

Ed Malone, the Diocesan Communications Director asked about sending a questionnaire with the next Sunday bulletin to all the parishioners of St. Francis inquiring about their level of satisfaction with the Parish. It would be a trial run of one for the Diocese. The Council agreed. Ed was given the green light to make it happen.

6) St. Francis Catholic Women's Association (CWA)

The monthly meeting of the CWA focussed on three issues: the planning for a girl's/women's softball team, the need for an emergency women's shelter in the town and the development of a third world program to adopt a single parent family.

7) St. Francis Men's Club:

The Men's Club continued in their snow clearing of sidewalks in the town especially for seniors, the maintenance of the two outdoor skating rinks and were preparing for spring parks clean up and maintenance.

8) The Samaritan Club:

This Club met again in St. Francis Rectory to celebrate food, prayer and the Eucharist. Jerome Nesbit led on addressing drug addiction among family and friends. It was a very moving experience.

9) The Developing Nations Program:

Fred and Thelma outlined their final plan: for this year only, they will be raffling off a holiday trailer and truck valued at $100,000 dollars. Every parish will be encouraged to sell tickets, priced at $25.00 each. The draw will be at the end of July. They hope to raise $100,000.00. With the proceeds, they hope to assemble a modular house over the winter with volunteer help, to raffle next Spring. Their goal to make $200,000. dollars.

10) The Interdenominational Committee:

This unusual committee is comprised of the local Anglican priest, the Reverend Claire Meadows; the local United Church minister, the Reverend Joan White; a Buddhist lay teacher, Ron Keating; a curious spiritual seeker, Peter Smith, Ed Malone, the Editor of the local newspaper, the Prairie News and Father Cam. They are promoting a town house painting program to beautify up the look of the community. They are also planning to institute a Dark House Program, where the local police will regularly check on houses where the owners or occupants are away.

11) The Town Expansion Plans:

The plan for the Town expansion was approved by Town Council. The approved plan will add six hundred and forty acres to its east boundary. A new Zoning Bylaw was also approved. Plans are underway for develop a Farmer's Market in the Town on weekends from the beginning of April to the end of October. The Town is inviting ideas for an annual summer festival, perhaps Heritage Days. Elaine Malone asked the Town to provide space for both a safe injection site and a drug overdose facility. The Town Administration assured her that they would be part of the expansion plans.

12) Annual priest's retreat:

During March, the Benedictines lead the annual priest's retreat. Their talks focussed on the key Benedictine spiritual principles of stability, obedience, prayer, work, hospitality and a commitment to the rule of St. Benedict. There were small group discussions twice a day on how these principles could influence our priestly lives. Archbishop Ben also attended this retreat.

## April report from the Diocese of Carthage to the Pope, Vatican Officials and the Canadian Bishops

1) The Deaconate Program:

   The April instruction focussed on the sacrament of the sick and the role of the deacon in a funeral ceremony. All participants now have the required Church vestments: albs, cinctures and stoles, and a ritual (to explain all the steps in the provision of each of the sacraments).

2) Diocesan Pastoral Council:

   The Diocese sadly announced the tragic sudden death of Father Mike. He died of a heart attack. The autopsy showed that it was a sudden death without any warning. Graciously, he would not have suffered. Archbishop Ben presided over an evening prayer service and a solemn Eucharistic Mass at St. Bonaventure, the Anglican Cathedral. Father Paul Campbell, a Benedictine in his late 70's, has agreed to replace Father Mike temporarily. Father Mike was a good friend to everyone. He will be sorely missed.

3) Diocesan Financial Committee:

   The Finance Committee is recommending that all financial matters in the Diocese be disclosed. All parishes will be asked to declare the value of the land and the Church buildings. There should be full disclosure of all monies contributed to the Church on an annual basis.

4) The Diocesan monthly priest's meeting:

   This month we discussed the development of a buddy system among the priests to avoid using alcohol as an escape from loneliness. This triggered a lengthy discussion on priests living in a community setting. It was a fruitful exchange. Next was a discussion of celebrating Mass in the family setting of a homes as a teaching tool particularly with young children. Concern was raised if these Masses encouraged taking too many short-cuts or liberties on how the Mass should be celebrated.

5) St Francis Parish Council:

The Parish Council met to plan for the inclusion of the twenty regular members of the United Church into St. Francis. Ed Malone, our Diocesan Communication Director suggested that all members of the Church, the Catholics, the Anglicans and United Church members should be consulted on this matter. He hoped to have the results available for the Diocesan report next month.

The planning continues for a Diocesan lottery by Fred and Thelma (they are suggesting three entry level modular homes of 1400 square feet that would be assembled in the community and then moved to a lot the winner selects. The draw is scheduled for October. They estimate that they can build these homes valued at $400,000.00 in the community at $115.00 a square foot thereby making a profit of approximately $339,000.00 per unit. The Diocese is considering a casino as well for next year. Our goal is to get our diocesan finances in order, maintenance plans in place for all the Churches and buildings and insurances up to date.

6) St. Francis Catholic Women's Association (CWA):

This women's group had organized a catechetical program for families where an abbreviated mass is celebrated in a family home at the time of an evening meal. The formula that included dinner, discussion of a gospel text and the Eucharist has been well received at St Francis, particularly in that it takes only one hour. Mabel inquired if this practice could be advocated in all the parishes.

Mabel also inquired if the CWA in the Diocese could take on the new program called "Adopt a Developing Third World Single Parent family." It was agreed.

7) St. Francis Men's Club:

Nothing to report this month.

8) The Samaritan Club:

This Club met again in St. Francis Rectory to celebrate food, Bible readings and the Eucharist. Raymond LeBois led a discussion on forgiveness among family and friends. It was a very challenging for some.

9) The Developing Nations Program:

Nothing to report this month. Plans are on hold until the Diocesan get its finances in order.

10) The Interdenominational Committee:

This committee's goal was to have twenty houses (20) painted last month but were only able to complete fifteen (15). Sergeant Ron Walker of the Royal Canadian Mounted Police (RCMP) have agreed to the Dark House Program.

11) The Town Expansion Plans:

Nothing to report this month.

## May report from the Diocese of Carthage to the Pope, Vatican Officials and the Canadian Bishops

1) The Deaconate Program:

   The May instruction focussed on distributing the Eucharist at Mass (lay people already distribute the Eucharist to home-bound Catholics.) and preaching homilies.

2) Diocesan Pastoral Council:

   The Council has asked Ed Malone and Mabel Armstrong to add the following to the monthly newsletter to each of the parishes. To enhance our children's appreciation of our faith, a) parents are encouraged to invite their parish priest to celebrate a home Eucharistic Mass, b) discuss our Catholic faith with your children over dinner. If you need help, please contact us. There are many good books, c) if you are attending Sunday Mass, review the homily with them on your way home, d) try to build a quiet time in your family for reflection with all electronic devices turned off, and e) start saying grace at the evening meal with intentions.

3) Diocesan Financial Committee:

   Nothing new to report.

4) St Francis Parish Council:

   The results of the consultation of all three congregations were unanimous. The members of the United Church would be welcome. Weekend liturgies would be as follows: there will be Catholic Masses on Saturday evening at 7:00 pm and Sunday at 10:00 am at St.

Francis and a Sunday Mass at St. Joseph's at 12:00 noon, Anglican Vespers at 5:00 pm Saturday and the Eucharistic Service on Sunday at 5:00 pm and the United Church Prayer Service on Sunday evening at 7:30 pm.

Ed presented the results of the Catholic satisfaction survey. Respondents were delighted to respond. A majority acknowledged that they lacked a basic knowledge of their faith, experienced conflicts between their Catholic beliefs and the secular world especially around sexual matters, they felt a major disconnect between the Church and the world and they wanted more spiritual guidance than moral direction.

5) St. Francis Catholic Women's Association:

   Nothing new to report.

6) St. Francis Men's Club:

   Nothing to report.

7) The Developing Nations Program:

   Nothing to report.

8) The Interdenominational Committee:

   Another 24 homes were painted this month.

9) The Town Expansion Plans:

   Nothing to report.

## June report from the Diocese of Carthage to the Pope, Vatican Officials and the Canadian Bishops

1) The Deaconate Program:

    The June instruction focussed on the explanation of the Catholic beliefs and the ordination to the Deaconate. Joan White and her wife Melody Summer are baptized conditionally in the event their original baptism was invalid.

2) Diocesan Pastoral Council:

    Ed Malone and Mabel Armstrong launched the Developing World Single Parent Adoption program diocesan wide through the newsletter. The CWA in the Diocese will coordinate this program from the St. Francis Parish.

3) The following committees cancelled their June meetings: the Diocesan Financial Committee, the St Francis Parish Council, the St. Francis Catholic Women's Association, the St. Francis Men's Club, the Developing Nations Program, and the Town Expansion Plan Committee.

4) The Interdenominational Committee:

    This committee reported that another fifteen homes and out buildings had been painted under this program.

## July report from the Diocese of Carthage to the Pope, Vatican Officials and the Canadian Bishops

Excerpt from the Prairies News (the local weekly newspaper) July 12 edition

On July 05, Archbishop Ben ordained fifteen members of the Diocese of Carthage to the deaconate at St. Bonaventure, the Anglican Cathedral, as part of a Eucharistic Service. They included Ned Armstrong, Colin and Marion McNeil, Liz McMillan, Ed and Elaine Malone, Reverend Joan White and her wife, Melody Summer, Simone Taylor and Jerome Atkins and his husband Raymond LeBois. In addition, another fifteen from the other 40 parishes in the Diocese were also ordained. They will now be able to support the current parish priests and baptize, confirm, preach, distribute communion and provide the sacrament to the sick.,

It was a celebratory event with many exuberant short speeches. Archbishop Ben thanked everyone for their time and commitment to both the Church and the community. Mabel was next. She exclaimed that she is still in shock that this ceremony occurred. She confessed that she did not think it would happen in her lifetime. This success has motivated her to continue to advocate for women's rights in the Church and society and then looking at the Archbishop and Father Cam, said that it would now be done "behind the scenes". The place broke into a polite applause and then a standing room ovation for her courage. Before she sat down, she thanked Ned for his undying support and encouragement over the past six months. She admitted that she could not have done it all without him covering her back. Ed then spoke thanking the parishioners at St. Francis for welcoming he and Elaine into their faith community. He expressed the hope that some day he will be able to write a book about this past year of extraordinary events at St. Francis. If such a book were to be possible, he would turn over all the profits to the Parish. Colin spoke next. He was so exuberant that he rambled incoherently, very uncharacteristic for a seasoned high school science teacher. Marion rescued him by thanking Mabel for her courage and stamina. Reverend Claire Meadows and Reverend Helen Jones in order thanked Archbishop Ben and Mabel for their leadership and courage that made this day possible and to the St Francis parishioners for making them feel so welcome. The celebration ended with a lunch of Mario's pizza and Caesar salads.

**Final journal entry:**

It is been one year of journals. They have helped me through a challenging first year of my priesthood. There is so much more I could tell you about these wonderful parishioners and now colleagues at the Diocesan level, but time does not permit. My plan going forward is to keep up my daily mantras practice, brief morning meditations and late evenings reflections where I can acknowledge and thank my loving Father in heaven for His many daily blessings. I plan on continuing my Tuesday scripture studies with the Anglicans, and my short stays with the Benedictines where I can recharge my batteries. But I will not be publishing my future journals. Thank you for your attention. Best wishes and blessings. Cam Walker, Catholic priest.

## ACKNOWLEDGEMENTS

The author wishes to thank the many family and friends who reviewed this manuscript and offer many helpful suggestions.

The author wishes to acknowledge the use of the following reference materials in developing this story:

1. Abraham J. Heschel, *The Prophets* (Harper & Row, 1963).
2. André Louf, OCSO, *In The School of Contemplation*, trans. Paul Rowe (Liturgical Press, 2015).
3. Barbara E. Reid, *The Gospel According to Matthew*, New Collegeville Bible Commentary (Liturgical Press, 2005).
4. Brother John of Taizé, *The Pilgrim God; A Biblical Journey* (Portland, OR: Pastoral Press, 1985).
5. Carol J. Dempsey, *Amos, Hosea, Micah, Nahum, Zephaniah, Habakkuk*, New Collegeville Bible Commentary (Liturgical Press, 2013).
6. Collegeville Bible Commentary: New Testament, gen. ed. Robert J. Karris (Liturgical Press, 1992).
7. Esther De Waal, *Seeking God: The Way of St. Benedict* (Liturgical Press, 1984).
8. Eugene H. Peterson, *The Message: The Bible in Contemporary Language* (NavPress, 2018).

9. Jacques Loew, *Face to Face with God: The Bible's Way to Prayer*, trans. Alan Neame (Darton, Longman & Todd, 1977).
10. Joan E. Cook, *Genesis*, New Collegeville Bible Commentary (Liturgical Press, 2010).
11. Living with Christ, Novalis Publishers, Toronto, Canada
12. Michael Duggan, *The Consuming Fire: A Christian Guide to the Old Testament* (Our Sunday Visitor, 2010).
13. Michael E. Patella, *The Gospel According to Luke*, New Collegeville Bible Commentary (Liturgical Press, 2005).
14. Patrick J. Hartin, *James, First Peter, Jude, Second Peter*, New Collegeville Bible Commentary (Liturgical Press, 2006).
15. Scott M. Lewis, *The Gospel According to John and the Johannine Letters*, New Collegeville Bible Commentary (Liturgical Press, 2005).
16. *The Harper Collins Study Bible including the Apocryphal Deuterocanonical Books*: New Revised Standard Version, student ed., gen. ed. Harold W. Attridge. (New York: Harper Collins, 2006).
17. *The Oblate Life*, ed. Gervase Holdaway (Liturgical Press, Collegeville Press, 1988).

The author takes full responsibility for any errors or omissions in the text. The author wants to unequivocally state to the reader that this is a book of fiction, developed in my very active imagination. Any resemblance to any person living or dead is purely coincidental.

## RECOMMENDED READINGS

For those readers who may be offended that my two volumes are critical of the Catholic Church, I have discussed below a number of authors, whom I have enjoyed reading over the years. These works focus on the Catholic Church and the life and work of Catholic priests. All are fiction and are considered classics.

1. Graham Greene (1904-1991) was born in England. His early employment was in newspapers, including the *Times* and the *Spector.* He was a film critic and a literary editor before becoming a prolific writer. He wrote novels, short stories, travel books, essays, plays, biographies, children's books and an autobiography. He became a Catholic in 1926 and visited Mexico in 1938 to report on the religious persecution there.

    I wish to draw your attention to one of his books, based on his Mexican experience titled, *The Power and the Glory,* originally published in 1940. In the 1930s, the Catholic Church was outlawed in Mexico. Priests were murdered unless they denied their faith and got married.

    In a poor, remote state in Southern Mexico, a paramilitary group had taken power. This story is about a weak, alcoholic priest who is on the run. With the police closing in on him and his life on the line, he is haunted by his mistakes; his fathering a child, his alcoholism and his fear of martyrdom. Despite these personal problems, he continues to serve those who request his help as he struggles to his Calvary and crucifixion. John Updike described this novel as Graham Greene's masterpiece.

2. C. F. Powers (1917-1999) was an American novelist and short story writer, who drew his inspiration from developments in the Catholic Church. Born and raised a Catholic, he was a conscientious objector during World War II. While not a priest, he is known for having been able to write about the priestly culture. His most famous novel, *Morte d'Urban*, won the National Book Award in 1963.

3. Andrew Greeley (1928-2013). Father Greeley was born into a large, Irish Catholic family in Chicago, Illinois. While never a parish priest, he became a sociologist, journalist and popular writer. As a sociologist, he published influential academic books in the 1960s and 1970s focusing on the Catholic Church in the United States. He argued that the imagery of Catholicism leads to a vital practice of it. The statues, the stained glass in churches and the stories of the Bible enhance the spiritual lives of ordinary Catholics. Catholicism is a religion of religious metaphors.

His fiction focused on the Catholic Church, parish life and priests who broke the law of celibacy. His treatment of sexuality in his novels was considered very controversial.

4.  Morris West (1916-1999), was born in Australia. He was a Catholic novelist and playwright best known for his novels *The Devil's Advocate* (1959), *The Shoes of the Fisherman* (1963) and *The Clowns of God* (1981). His novels often addressed the role of the papacy in international politics. In *The Shoes of the Fisherman*, he described the election and career of a Ukrainian who became pope fifteen years before the election of the Polish Pope, John Paul II. I the sequel, *The Clowns of God*, his novel describes a pope who resigns from the papacy to live in seclusion some thirty-two years before Pope Benedict's resignation in 2013.

5.  Ignazio Silone (1900-1978) was the pseudonym for Secondo Tranquilly. He was an underground political organizer during the 1930s Fascist regime in Italy. As a member of the outlawed communist party, he risked his life as an organizer. He was ultimately smuggled into Switzerland where he lived and wrote returning to Italy in 1944. He wrote two amazing books; *Bread and Wine* and *The Story of a Humble Christian*.

    *Bread and Wine* is a semibiographical story of the return to Italy of an outlawed political organizer. To protect him while he recovers from an illness and regains his strength, his friends give him the attire of a priest as his disguise. He is given a black cassock, a wide black hat, and a breviary (a priest's prayer book). He travels in a remote part of Italy and presents himself as someone recovering from a lengthy illness. To the requests of the Italians for his spiritual help celebrating Mass or hearing confessions, he feigns that he is not strong enough to provide such services.

*The Story of a Humble Christian* is a novel of Pietro Angelerio (a.k.a. Pietro da Morrone, Peter of Morrone and Peter Celestine (1215-1296). He became a Benedictine monk and then a hermit. He also started a religious order called the Celestines, a branch of the Benedictines. During a papal election that failed to elect a pope, he was elected on July 05, in 1294 in absentia in the Catholic Church's last non-conclave election. He became Pope Celestine V, and in addition, he was the ruler of the Papal States. He found the duties of the pope very difficult. The Catholic Church at the time was very corrupt. In addition to selling indulgences that removed temporal punishment from sins committed on earth, priests were illiterate and had difficulty carrying out their priestly duties. Priests and nuns, despite their vows of chastity, engaged in sexual relationships, bishops and abbots lived luxurious lives, and some popes fathered and raised children.

Pope Celestine V found the papal duties unmanageable and impossible. After five months, on December 13, 1294, he resigned. His successor, Pope Boniface VIII put him in prison where he died in 1296.

In my opinion, this novel is another example of Silone's themes, that portrays the lives of Christians who struggle to live the teachings of Christ in a world that is disinterested and even hostile to the Christian message.

## IN PRAISE OF VOLUME I

The writing is captivating. The stories and the characters are captivating. I cared about them. A breath of fresh air on controversial topics. A manual on how the powers of listening and wanting to help others can unify communities.
-Sergio Martinez

A refreshing, provocative and readable account of ministry in Church and the challenges facing priests and the laity today. Jack's book highlights in a unique way the need of the hierarchy of the Church to consider change or adjustment to some current Church practices while maintaining a fidelity to the teachings of Jesus.
-Maureen Gagnon

Jack has presented a fresh and attractive vision of the Catholic Church. I hope Pope Francis gets a copy of this book.
-Carole Perkins.

Manufactured by Amazon.ca
Bolton, ON

33320347R00157